BIKING OURAY

MARCUS WILSON

PRESS

RIDGWAY, COLORADO

Published by Wayfinder Press
P.O. Box 217
Ridgway, Colorado 81432

Design,
Editing, Typography, Maps:
Pat Wilson

Printed by Country Graphics, Ridgway, CO
U.S.A.

Photography:
Judy Kohin by Primoz Kotnik
Falls and *Seated Bikers* by Marcus Wilson

ISBN 0-943727-16-2

*The only Zen you find on the tops of mountains
is the Zen you bring up there.*

- Robert Persig

To Billie, Woody and Kocis'

*Special thanks and love to
graphic designer, typesetter, cartographer, editor and
all-around critic and motivator, Pat Wilson.*

PREFACE

Any form of activity such as biking is inherently adventuresome, if not dangerous. You must be aware and maintain control at all times. Your fate is in your own hands, and is also controlled by the brain beneath your helmet.

I have taken all the rides described in this book and returned relatively unscathed. You, however, are on your own. Don't blame me if weather conditions are not ideal, if road conditions change, if new rocks appear, if a runaway Jeep hits you, or you descend a 60 degree slope on a flimsy, imitation mountain bike without a helmet. To me, my directions are simple and straightforward. To you, they are only a guide; they must be interpreted. Always be prepared; remember the words of Oscar Wilde, "The pure and simple truth is rarely pure and never simple."

CONTENTS

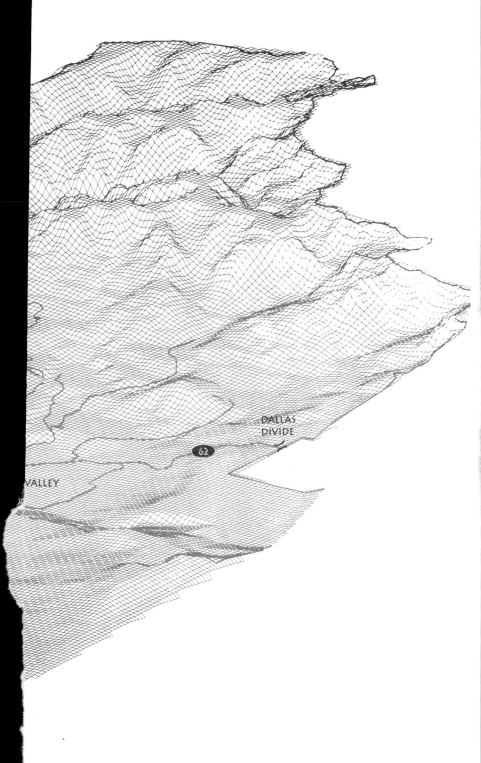

DALLAS
DIVIDE

62

VALLEY

USING THE GUIDE

Always wear a helmet. Check your bike before riding: brakes and tires especially. Carry enough water and extra clothing for all weather conditions. At high altitudes snow can, and does, occur every month of the year. At least be prepared for rain during the summer. Carry tools. Although none of these rides will take you beyond walking distance of civilization, it can be a long walk if you are pushing or carrying a bike. And remember you may be riding at an elevation far beyond what you are used to. Be self-sufficient but don't travel alone. Tread lightly: take only pictures and leave nothing.

The description of each ride begins with a general discussion of the ride, an elevation/distance graph, a map, time of ride (I do not stop except for matters involving liquids), trail terrain, and degree of difficulty. The determination of the degree of difficulty is based upon a combination of all of these factors. Your physical condition and level of acclimatization must be combined with these factors.

Most of the rides are in the 10-15 mile range but are grouped so that by combining rides you can pedal all day if you like. I indicate mileage, elevation, time riding, and appropriate comments at regular intervals. The degree of difficulty is shown by a rating of one to five bike pedal symbols 🚴🚴🚴, with one being the easiest. The start points are described after the bullet • symbol. Read through the entire ride description so that you are aware of the vagueries of each ride before you begin.

All elevation readings are based on an altimeter reading of 6970 feet from the Ridgway Town Park or 7620 feet at the Ouray Hot Springs Pool. These numbers are relative. They are only a guide to gain or loss, not to an exact measure

1

of elevation. Be aware of the possibility of altitude sickness. It will usually appear 12 to 36 hours after reaching a new altitude greater that 8,000 feet. Symtoms include headache, nausea, dizziness, loss of appetite, fatigue, coordination loss, and insomnia. The potential for altitude sickness increases with over-exertion in the first 24 hours, a too rapid ascent, dehydration, the use of drugs or alcohol (respiratory depressants), and unfavorable genes. Note: gender and/or physical fitness have no effect on your potential for altitude sickness. Treatments include pain medicines for headaches (avoid sedatives), descent and rest. For this or any other medical emergency call 911.

Most rides take advantage of what I feel is the best way to ride: do the most work first so that you can look forward to the fun, the descent.

As you ride always be aware of the possibility of animals running out in front of you. Marmots, chipmunks, squirrels, badgers, and the ubiquitous deer have all altered my course at one time or another. Hitting a deer at speeds up to 30 miles per hour would ruin a good ride.

Always respect private property. Leave gates the way you find them. Do not venture into wilderness areas where bicycles are prohibited. Relinquish the right-of-way to everyone and everything.

I have assumed that you have ridden something beyond a stationary bicycle. The vast majority of these rides do not require more than basic biking skills. For any ride, however, keep in mind the following comments: when descending keep your weight back and low; when climbing, your weight should be forward. Do not over-brake or you may be flipped. They only work when you are moving. When sidehilling keep your inside pedal up. Never tie clothing or other articles to your bike that can come loose and jam your tires. If falling let go of your bike. Above all, maintain control.

I. Pleasant Valley Map

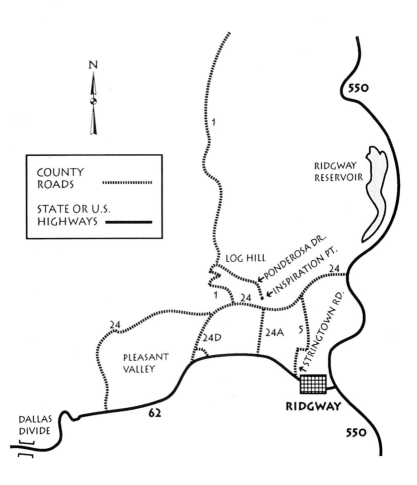

1. String Town Road

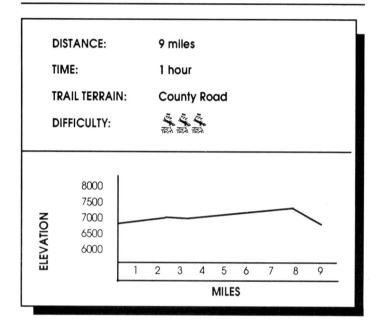

DISTANCE:	9 miles
TIME:	1 hour
TRAIL TERRAIN:	County Road
DIFFICULTY:	

This ride is 9 miles long over county roads with very little elevation change. It should take approximately 1 hour to ride and will give you a good view of the Uncompahgre Valley from the base of Log Hill Mesa. It also gives you access to many other rides, including Log Hill, Pleasant Valley, Ridgway Reservoir, and Dallas Creek. Llamas, camels, and Dennis Weaver are also featured.

•Begin at the Ridgway Town Park at an elevation of 6970 feet. Ride west on Clinton St. (the street in front of the Post Office) for five blocks past the baseball field on your left to Amelia Street. Turn right and head north past the Ridgway School on what will become County Road 5. This is called String Town Road.

1 mile mark: elevation 6990, Sundance art foundry and sculpture garden on your left.

A rutting camel at the Double LL Corral Ranch.

Continue north as the road turns hard right heading east at the 1.4 mile mark. Up a slight rise to an elevation of 7020 you get a nice view of Ridgway and the valley up to Ouray to the north and the Cimarron Range with Chimney Peak and Courthouse Mountain to the east. Follow the road as it turns north.

2 mile mark: elevation 7040, you have just passed the entrance to the Eagle Hill Ranch.

Eagle Hill Ranch is an equestrian subdivision. It is one of the many responses now taking place in the county to an ever-expanding problem of this area and of the whole country: the second-homeless. Continue on the road as it heads north, then east, and then north again to a T-intersection. This is County Road 24.

2.5 mile mark: elevation 6970, intersection County Road 5 and County Road. 24, with Dallas Creek on your left. Approximately 15 minutes into the ride.

Turn left. (If you turn right, about 9/10 of a mile is the bike and foot path entrance to the Ridgway Reservoir.) You are heading west on Road 24 along the base of Log Hill Mesa. Up the road a bit (3 mile mark, elevation 7030) you'll see a large log home on you left along with a good view of the valley and the Sneffels Range.

3.7 mile mark: elevation 7080, intersection with County Road 24A on your left.

If you're tired, sprained an ankle, or have a hangover you can return to Ridgway quickly on this road via Highway 62 (about 2.6 miles). Otherwise continue straight west toward the Weaver residence.

4.8 mile mark: elevation 7150, 30 minutes into the ride, intersection where County Road 24 turns left as County Road 1 continues up to Log Hill Mesa.

Just before this intersection you'll see a llama ranch on your left with camels, (two-humped) Bactrians, buffalo, and, of course, llamas. This is the Double LL Corral llama ranch. At the intersection you turn left and continue on County Road 24. If you go straight you are in for a steep climb which is described on the Log Hill ride. At the intersection you will see an entry arch that says "Sunridge." This is Dennis Weaver's used tire, crushed aluminum can, passive solar, solar voltaic 2nd or 3rd home. The thought of a $3 million dollar energy-efficient home somehow seems to miss the point but I'm

THE POWER OF ACCURATE OBSERVATION IS COMMONLY CALLED CYNICISM BY THOSE WHO HAVE NOT GOT IT.

-GEORGE BERNARD SHAW

sure there are those that also call Trump pretentious.

Continue on Road 24 as it crosses a bridge over Dallas Creek. You are heading southwest up a small hill with Dennis' house, tipi, and pyramid on your right. At the top you'll pass two trailer homes on your right and re-enter the real world.

5.7 mile mark: elevation 7160, 40 minutes into the ride, intersection where Road 24 turns right to Pleasant Valley. Continue straight.

You are now on County Road 24D. Continue to the next intersection at the 6 mile mark. Either way brings you to Highway 62 and the return to Ridgway. If you are not partial to highway riding retrace your route to Ridgway. I turn left and head for Highway 62.

6.3 mile mark: elevation 7180, 46 minutes, intersection of County Road 24D and State Highway 62.

Turn left for a quick trip back to Ridgway on the highway. This is a good place for some speed riding but remember that the general rule for most drivers is "How close can I get to a bike rider without scratching my car" or at least that's how it feels sometimes. Stay to the right. This is one of the few highways in this area with a wide shoulder. Take advantage of it. At the 7.5 mile mark you will come to the intersection of Highway 62 and Road 24A to Log Hill which we mentioned earlier at its northern end. Continue straight.

8.1 mile mark: elevation 7220, 55 minutes into ride, top of the hill overlooking Ridgway. An excellent view of the valley from here.

Follow the highway down the hill back to the Town Park. You can get good speed going down this hill but remember there is a school speed zone at the bottom and, as I rode this, I saw two gold eagles on this hill. Return to Town Park to finish a ride of 9 miles in about an hour.

2. Log Hill

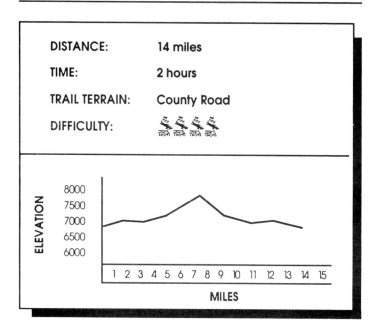

DISTANCE:	14 miles
TIME:	2 hours
TRAIL TERRAIN:	County Road
DIFFICULTY:	(four symbols)

ELEVATION
8000
7500
7000
6500
6000

1 2 3 4 5 6 7 8 9 10 11 12 13 14 15

MILES

•Follow the directions for the String Town Road Ride. At the 4.8 mile mark you come to the intersection of County Road 24 and County Road 1. Instead of turning left you continue straight up, and I mean up, the road to the top of Log Hill. At the top you will find Fairway Pines Country Club, restaurant, athletic club, golf course, and many biking alternatives. The total round trip from Ridgway to Log Hill and back is a little over 14 miles. From this intersection it is only 2.2 miles to the top, but the elevation gain is almost 800 feet.

4.9 mile mark: you will pass the Bryant house on your left with a houseboat out front that will be on the Ridgway Reservoir sooner or later.

5 mile mark: elevation 7240, 35 minutes from Ridgway. You are now leaving the Ridgway Fire District. The land

Scenic view of the Sneffels Range one-third of the way up Log Hill.

along this road continues to be developed. Combined with the expansive plans of the developers of Fairway Pines, the result is an on-going increase in traffic on this road. This has resulted in an outcry for road improvements which in turn will result in increased traffic which will produce more outcries: a simple definition of growth.

> **SUBURBIA IS WHERE**
>
> **THE DEVELOPER**
>
> **BULLDOZES OUT THE**
>
> **TREES, THEN NAMES**
>
> **THE STREETS**
>
> **AFTER THEM.**
>
> -BILL VAUGHN

5.5 mile mark: elevation 7420, 41 minutes into the ride, as you turn left into the first major switchback views of Pleasant Valley and the Sneffels Range begin to open up.

6 mile mark: elevation 7620.

6.2 mile mark: elevation 7710, 49 minutes, a small turnout at this point provides a good observation perch before the road turns back into the trees and the final leg to the top. At the 6.3 mile mark you see a house to your right on the escarpment, the level to which you aspire.

6.5 mile mark: elevation 7810, 58 minutes.

7 mile mark: elevation 7920, the top, turn right at the intersection and you will see tennis courts and the club: Fairway Pines Country Club. Have lunch or dinner or brunch on weekends. Perhaps take a soak (call ahead to be sure non-members are welcome) or talk to a salesperson, either, a relaxing experience.

3. INSPIRATION POINT

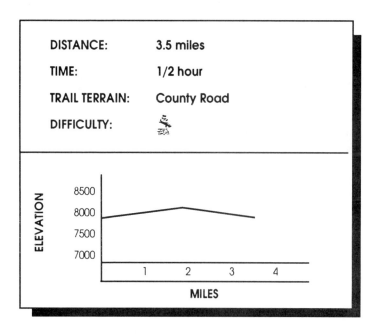

DISTANCE:	3.5 miles
TIME:	1/2 hour
TRAIL TERRAIN:	County Road
DIFFICULTY:	

ELEVATION

8500
8000
7500
7000

1   2   3   4

MILES

This ride totals only 3.5 miles and rates only one foot pedal on the difficulty scale. Beginning at Fairway Pines Golf and Country Club it takes you to an excellent viewing point, on the Log Hill escarpment, of the Uncompahgre and Pleasant valleys. It can also be the jumping off point for any length of ride exploring the many county roads of Log Hill.

• At the golf club at the intersection of County Road 1 and Ponderosa Drive (see Log Hill ride) head east. Elevation is 7920. Passing some large

GOLF IS A GAME IN WHICH

YOU CLAIM THE

PRIVILEGES OF AGE, AND

RETAIN THE PLAYTHINGS

OF CHILDHOOD.

-SAMUEL JOHNSON

An inspirational view at the Point.

piles of dirt and rocks on your left you should see part of the golf course. Up a hill on your right is the Log Hill Volunteer Fire Department. You are on Ponderosa Drive.

.3 mile mark: the intersection with Canyon on your left; continue straight.

.5 mile mark: elevation 7980.

1 mile mark: elevation 7990; come to the intersection with Pine on your right. Turn right and follow Pine as it circles south and east.

1.45 mile mark: elevation 8030; turn right on Tower.

1.75 mile mark: you have come to a dead end and Inspiration Point. Elevation 8090. An excellent view of Dallas Divide to Ouray; from Sneffels to the Cimarrons. Retrace you steps to the intersection of Pine and Tower.

2 mile mark: elevation 8030; the intersection of Pine and Tower. Go straight on Tower until your reach Ponderosa. Turn left and return to the Club House.

3.5 mile mark: back at the Club.

4. PLEASANT VALLEY

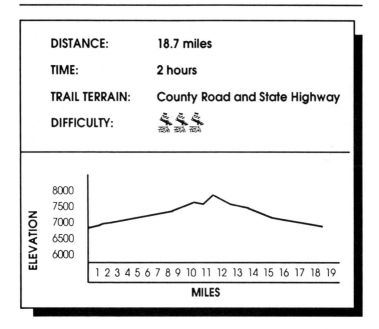

DISTANCE: 18.7 miles

TIME: 2 hours

TRAIL TERRAIN: County Road and State Highway

DIFFICULTY:

ELEVATION

8000
7500
7000
6500
6000

1 2 3 4 5 6 7 8 9 10 11 12 13 14 15 16 17 18 19

MILES

By following the directions for the String Town ride 5.7 miles along County Roads 5 and 24 you will come to the intersection of Roads 24 and 24D. Instead of continuing on 24D to Highway 62 and back to Ridgway you turn right and head west on Road 24. The round trip back to this point is approximately 10 miles. Back to Ridgway from this point through Pleasant Valley is approximately 13 miles. This is a beautiful ride through a valley aptly named. The views of the Sneffels Range are magnificent. The ride is all on County Roads or State Highway. The elevation gain is about 700 feet but takes 6 miles and is not strenuous. The return ride is all downhill and exhilarating. If you start in Ridgway, follow the String Town Ride instructions, and then branch off on this ride. The round trip comes to almost nineteen miles.

•Starting point of County Roads 24 and 24D is at an elevation of 7160. Taking County Road 24 you immediately

Pastoral Pleasant Valley.

cross a bridge over Dallas Creek, heading west. As you ride slowly up and away from Dallas Creek you see the Sneffels Range to your left and to the right you see Log Hill Mesa as it merges with the Uncompahgre Plateau.

2 mile mark: elevation 7360; 17 minutes into ride. You are riding along the north edge of the valley with a stock pond on your left. As I ride today I see a horse-drawn trashing machine working in a field to my left and circular bales of hay dot the landscape. However, agriculture is slowly being replaced by residences and subdivisions. Maybe slowly is the wrong word.

3 mile mark: elevation 7420; 25 minutes. Just before the 3 mile mark the road angles left and heads south. At the 3 mile mark you again cross Dallas Creek.

3.6 mile mark: elevation 7480; 28 minutes. On your left is a large hay corral at the top of a small rise. Here you'll get an excellent 360 degree view of the valley, the Sneffels Range, and the Uncompahgre Plateau.

4 mile mark: elevation 7530; 35 minutes. As you come up a small rise a ranch with old out-buildings will be on your right. Continue to climb.

4.5 mile mark: elevation 7750; 39 minutes into ride. Quickly drop down to a "T" intersection to the left of which you will see a sign proclaiming a Colorado Centennial Farm. Designated as such by the Colorado Department of Agriculture and the Colorado Historical Society, this is the Fournier Ranch, owned by the same family for over a hundred years. Turn left to the Fournier Ranch if you are friends of theirs and they are expecting you, otherwise turn right and continue south on the road.

5 mile mark: elevation 7620; 45 minutes. At the 5.2 mile mark you are into the final climb.

5.8 mile mark: elevation 7820; 55 minutes. You are at the intersection of Road 24 and State Highway 62. For less traffic turn around and retrace your route. For some speed work and glimpses of famous landholdings turn left on Highway 62 (if you turn right you will be headed up hill for about four miles to the top of Dallas Divide — the Telluride route.) All the land to your right as you quickly descend is part of the Double RL Ranch, owned by fashion czar Ralph Lauren (his property extends almost to the top of Dallas Divide).

> IT IS A KIND OF SPIRITUAL SNOBBERY THAT MAKES PEOPLE THINK THEY CAN BE HAPPY WITHOUT MONEY.
>
> - ALBERT CAMUS

6.3 mile mark: a stock pond on your right lies just north and up the hill from the Lauren residence (you can't see it from the road so I'll describe it). It is a large, log structure with the many accoutrements befitting a wealthy design magnate, including a natural rock swimming pool, the rocks of which were color-selected by Ralph — very chappish. A little farther on you'll see a group of buildings on the right which comprises the cooking facilities and auxiliary bunkhouse for Lauren's visits. The Double RL Ranch has replaced

Mount Sneffels as seen from County Road 24.

the historic Marie Scott Ranch, and has done an admirable job of preserving this property and continuing it as a working ranch.

6.9 mile mark: elevation 7610; the intersection of Highway 62 and Ouray County Road 9. This is a National Forest Access road, West Dallas Road. It travels through the Double RL Ranch to the Uncompahgre National Forest, a ride described in Trail 6. West Dallas Road.

7.6 mile mark: on your right are the administration buildings, barns, and insemination facilities of the Double RL, on your left is Marie Scott's old, white homestead.

8.3 mile mark: elevation 7470; the intersection of Highway 62 and County Road 7, the Dallas Creek National Forest Access. Locally called East Dallas Creek, this road travels about 9 miles back to Willow Swamps where a trail leads to Blue Lakes, alpine lakes just below Mt. Sneffels. This road is described in Trail 5 Dallas Creek.

9.8 mile mark: intersection of Highway 62 and County Road 24D. By turning left you can return to your starting point or continue straight on the highway back to Ridgway. About one hour and ten minutes for the trip to this point.

II. DALLAS CREEK MAP

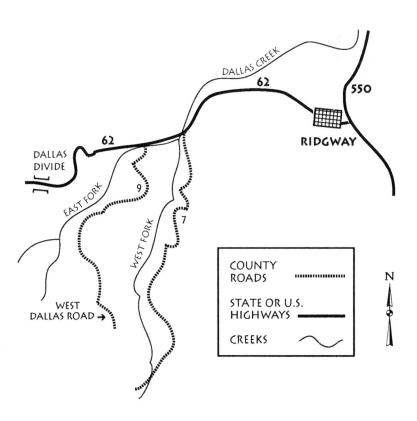

5. DALLAS CREEK

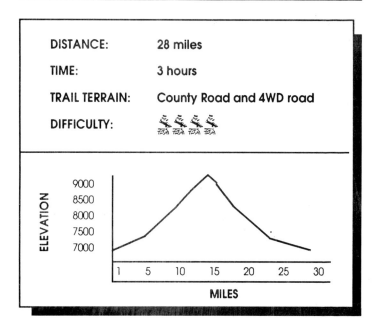

DISTANCE:	28 miles
TIME:	3 hours
TRAIL TERRAIN:	County Road and 4WD road
DIFFICULTY:	

Locally known as East Dallas Creek, this ride begins in Ridgway, travels along Highway 62 and a county road for a round trip of about 28 miles. You can drive to the intersection of Highway 62 and County Road 7 and begin your trip there and reduce the mileage to 19 miles. The county road passes through private property as it accesses the Uncompahgre National Forest. It is uphill most of the way. It is generally an easy rise except for one section of less than a mile. There are many custom homes to be seen on this road and the views, as always, are excellent.

• Beginning at the Ridgway Town Park at an elevation of 6970 either ride or drive 4.6 miles west on Highway 62 to County Road 7, Dallas Creek National Forest Access, elevation 7420. Turn left here and follow the road. Mileage readings will begin from this point.

Wolford's cow camp along Dallas Creek.

.4 mile mark: as you come to a "Y" stay left following the directions on the sign that says Uncompahgre National Forest. Elevation 7440. Cross a cattle guard.

1 mile mark: elevation 7500; you are riding above and to the left of the East Fork of Dallas Creek.

1.5 mile mark: elevation 7560.

2 mile mark: elevation 7620.

2.2 mile mark: you come to another "Y" in the road. Stay right, cross another cattle guard and follow sign proclaiming Uncompahgre National Forest.

2.5 mile mark: elevation 7750; 25 minutes into ride. Starting the major climb of this ride, a series of switchbacks.

3 mile mark: elevation 7850; still climbing but not as steeply

3.5 mile mark: elevation 8010; 40 minutes into ride.

3.7 mile mark: small stock pond on your left.

4 mile mark: elevation 8080; cross a cattle guard and through a double gate leaving the Ridgway Fire District.

5 mile mark: elevation 8320; 55 minutes into ride. Just before the 5 mile mark cross another cattle guard and pass through a double gate.

5.5 mile mark: elevation 8440; it has been all uphill so far but for the switchbacks not too tough. Still climbing.

6 mile mark: elevation 8610; another cattle guard brings us to the top of this section.

6.5 mile mark: elevation 8730; beginning to drop down to Willow Swamps.

7.5 mile mark: elevation 8990; 80 minutes into ride. Swamp area is to your right and looking straight south down the road is Mt. Sneffels.

7.7 mile mark: another cattle guard and double gate marks the entrance to the National Forest.

8 mile mark: elevation 9080.

8.5 mile mark: elevation 9110; you see a sign reading "Your National Forest Help Keep It Clean." You are at Willow Swamps; there's even a bathroom if you can find it. Continue on the road.

Willow Swamps.

8.7 mile mark: you come to a bridge crossing East Dallas Creek. As you have seen, there are many camp sites in the area plus an abundance of roads and trails available for bike exploring. **9 mile mark:** elevation 9150; 95 minutes. At the 9.35 mile mark you will end at the Blue Lakes Trailhead. This trail is in a wilderness area and therefore not open to bikes but it is recommended as a short, beautiful hike. It is 3.5 miles to the lower Blue Lakes and 6 miles to Blue Lake Pass which takes you over to Yankee Boy Basin and Ouray, or return to highway 62 or Ridgway.

6. WEST DALLAS ROAD

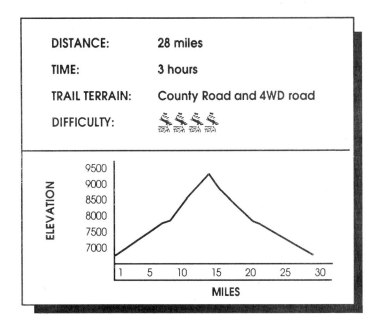

DISTANCE: 28 miles

TIME: 3 hours

TRAIL TERRAIN: County Road and 4WD road

DIFFICULTY: 🚵 🚵 🚵 🚵

ELEVATION (9500, 9000, 8500, 8000, 7500, 7000) vs MILES (1, 5, 10, 15, 20, 25, 30)

This ride is along a county road that winds through private property (Ralph Lauren's Double RL Ranch) to the Uncompahgre National Forest. If you begin in Ridgway the round-trip distance is 28 miles; from the intersection of Highway 62 and the county road (number 9) the roundtrip is 16 miles. It is a lightly traveled road and quite scenic. The shorter round-trip will take about 2 hours; the longer a little more than three hours. Elevation gain from the highway intersection is about 1850 feet making the uphill section of this ride quite strenuous. However, it is well worth the effort.

• From Ridgway Town Park follow State Highway 62 west for six miles to County Road 9. There will be a sign stating National Forest Access West Dallas Road. Turn left here and follow the road. There is a second sign stating that private property borders the road for the next 7.5 miles. Please respect the private property, if not the mileage measurement.

You will immediately pass under a log arch that proclaims Double RL-the famous Ralph and Ricky Lauren Ranch. Beginning elevation is 7640. This is a working ranch so keep an eye out for all the designer cattle. Right after the arch you will come to a gate at the creek. Go through the gate leaving it open or closed as you found it.

.4 mile mark: a fork in the road, stay left.

.5 mile mark: elevation 7670; as you round a bend you will get a good view of the Sneffels Range.

.7 mile mark: another fork, stay to the right (the left turn goes down through hay fields and pastures).

1 mile mark: elevation 7730.

1.2 mile mark: another fork, stay right.

1.5 mile: elevation 7870; 15 minutes into the ride from the intersection.

1.7 mile mark: elevation 7890; there is a stock pond off to your left. There is another fork beyond the pond, stay left.

1.9 mile mark: there is a small mileage sign that says "2" at this point. Just before this sign you will cross a cattle guard at an elevation of 7910. You will soon begin a pretty steep hill.

2.5 mile mark: elevation 8140; 25 minutes, still climbing.

2.7 mile mark: elevation 8220; about a tenth of a mile farther after turning sharply right you will crest the hill and find yourself riding on bedrock and notice the road is now paralleling a gorge to your right, West Dallas Creek.

3 mile mark: elevation 8270; 34 minutes into ride along the gorge.

3.2 mile mark: elevation 8320; a sign stating "Please stay on roads entering public lands."

3.5 mile mark: elevation 8410; 39 minutes.

3.8 mile mark: leaving public lands.

3.9 mile mark: elevation 8500; small road sign says "4."

4 mile mark: elevation 8520; 45 minutes.

4.4 mile mark: elevation 8580; there is a stock pen on your right. On your left is a small cabin that is called the Vance. Looking south-southeast you can see Mt. Sneffels just above the road as it continues south.

4.5 mile mark: elevation 8600; 52 minutes.

4.8 mile mark: elevation 8610; you will pass a road on your left that would take you to the Back of the Moon house if you were Ralph Lauren. Stay right on the road.

5 mile mark: elevation 8670; 57 minutes. Just beyond this point you may be able to discern an overgrown driveway leading off to the left. This was the driveway to the Burden house before it was purchased by the Laurens. It was a huge log structure that Ralph had de-constructed because it ruined his view — so the story goes.

> GIVE ONE MAN A
>
> LECTURE ON MORALITY
>
> AND ANOTHER A
>
> SHILLING, AND SEE
>
> WHICH WILL RESPECT
>
> YOU MOST.
>
> -SAMUEL JOHNSON

5.2 mile mark: elevation 8700; crossing a cattle guard you have a good view of the western half of the Sneffels Range.

5.5 mile mark: elevation 8800; 63 minutes.

6 mile mark: elevation 8950.

County Road 9 and the entrance to the Double RL Ranch.

6.15 mile mark: elevation 9010; 72 minutes. Sign marking the entrance to the National Forest.

6.65 mile mark: elevation 9190; the road becomes very rough. Up to this point the road was passable by any vehicle, now it is four-wheel drive only.

6.8 mile mark: elevation 9240; 80 minutes. Road has leveled by this point as you come to a small open area, continue.

6.9 mile mark: come to 3-way fork. Take the middle road; the right fork swings back to meet the middle road while the left fork is a shorter version of the road we are on which travels to the Sneffels Wilderness. This is an area with many camping possibilities and a favorite with hunters.

7 mile mark: elevation 9200; cross the West Dallas Creek, which you have been loosely paralleling this whole trip. Just after the creek come to a fork: to the right see a sign saying Dallas Trail #209, keep to the left.

6.2 mile mark: elevation 9220; Road continues through a large open area-two ruts with a grass median strip. The road then heads into the forest and is very rough.

7.65 mile mark: elevation 9320; an area filled with numerous downed trees with West Dallas Creek on your left.

8 mile mark: elevation 9480; end of the road. You will see a sign announcing Mt. Sneffels Wilderness, Uncompahgre National Forest Wilderness: closed to motorized vehicles, hang gliders, and bikes. Return to starting point. Remember to use caution on your return because high speeds can be achieved.

III. UNCOMPAHGRE VALLEY MAP

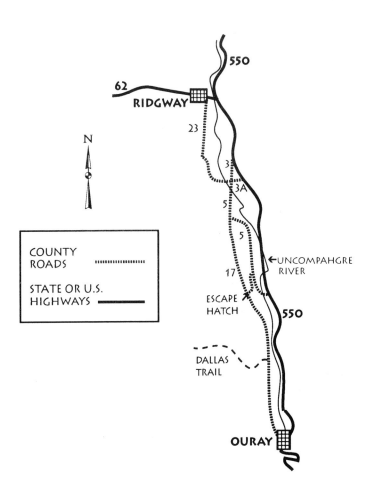

7. THE RIVER ROAD

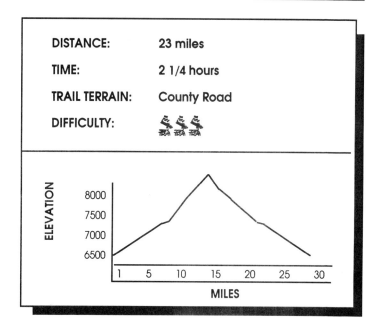

DISTANCE:	23 miles
TIME:	2 1/4 hours
TRAIL TERRAIN:	County Road
DIFFICULTY:	

This is the back road to Ouray. It is uphill all the way to Ouray but it is a gentle rise. It is an eleven and a half mile trip one way. Many times we will ride to Ouray for a brunch at the Bon Ton or the Piñon on a Sunday morning along with a soak in the hot springs pool because even with a full stomach the ride back is mostly coasting. It is also a very pretty ride with very little traffic, all on county roads. You may shorten this ride by taking the Orvis turn-off or the Idlewild Escape Hatch which are described later.

•Begin at the Ridgway Town Park at an elevation of 6970 and head south on Lena St., pass the Solar Ranches subdivision and onto County Road 23.

1 mile mark: elevation 7080 feet. The Elk River Ranch is on your right at the top of a small hill.

The San Juan Guest Ranch entrance.

Good viewing point up valley to Ouray. Slowly you descend as the road winds around on the west side of the valley. If you have begun your ride early enough in the day you can probably see a hot air balloon rising in the sky over your shoulder north to Ridgway belonging to San Juan Balloon Adventures of Ridgway.

2.4 mile mark: elevation 7100. A large boulder on your left, with a 45 degree angled crack running through it, is a favorite for the local marmots and squirrels. Also along this stretch I've seen eagles patrolling the escarpment to the west. I have been informed by the people of the Park Nursery, just down the road, that they are a common sight.

At the Park Nursery follow the road as it turns east and heads downhill toward the Uncompahgre River. Just before the bridge over the river at the 3.2 mile mark turn right following the road south toward the San Juan Guest Ranch which will be on your left at the 4.2 mile mark, elevation 7140, 27 minutes into the ride. If you want to shorten your ride continue across the bridge at the 3.2 mile mark for the Orvis Ride, described later.

When two worlds collide.

4.4 mile mark: elevation 7150. Just north of the San Juan Guest Ranch you will come to a fork. Keep to the right, cross the cattle guard and begin the major climb of the ride to Black Lake. There are great views of the valley on this section especially during the Fall when the valley trees, shrubs, and scrub oak begin to turn into "the Magic Carpet." The road to the left is a continuation of County Road 23 and the road to the right is Road 17. The road to the left is part of the Idlewild Escape Hatch which is described later.

5.2 mile mark: crossing a cattle guard. On both sides of the road you'll see paths that belong to a goat herd that range here. If you are lucky you might even cross paths with these friendly animals. Undoubtedly you will hear the tingle of goat's bells or the call of some marmots in this area, also known as whistle pigs.

5.5 mile mark: elevation 7230; 35 minutes into the ride. Cross a third cattle guard. One-half a mile further on you will cross a fourth cattle guard at an elevation of 7260 and the sub-division of Idlewild begins to show it's face down the hill to your left. You'll pass Pine Ridge Drive on your left where for some reason no parking is allowed. The elevation is 7300. Continue to climb.

6.2 mile mark: elevation 7330. Pass a large brown house on your right as the road swings left and intersects with a road on your left that heads downhill and is called Suzanne Lane. I call this the Idlewild Escape Hatch. The road goes through the Idlewild sub-division north along the Uncompahgre River and swings back along Road 23 to the San Juan Guest Ranch. By returning to Ridgway this way you will have a trip of about 14 miles. Continue straight to your right.

6.6 mile mark: elevation 7380. You will see Elk Ridge Trail on your right that leads to many roads up the side of the valley to Elk Meadows. This road is a steep long climb that intersects with many closed roads. It's work. Continue straight. Beyond Elk Ridge Trail you might notice a chain saw wood sculpture on your right depicting the tragedy that results when two species collide.

> THERE ARE TIMES
> WHEN YOU HAVE
> TO CHOOSE
> BETWEEN BEING
> HUMAN AND
> HAVING GOOD
> TASTE.
>
> -BERTOLT BRECHT

7.0 mile mark: elevation 7450; 52 minutes into the ride. You are at the top of a hill overlooking Black Lake. This isn't the top but it is still a very flat ride the rest of the way into Ouray. Looking west you can see many of the roads that are accessible from Elk Ridge Trail. As you leave Black Lake behind, you hug the side of the hill with the Uncompahgre River to your left, with Mt. Abrahms rising straight out of the road to the south. Elevation is 7480.

8.7 mile mark: elevation 7500. The road passes the beginning of the Dallas Trail to your right. This is the exit point of the Elk Meadows Ride described elsewhere. Continue up the road to where a bridge crosses the river on your left. This is highway 550 which connects Ouray and Ridgway (9.1 miles). Avoid the traffic and continue on the dirt road. to your right. The elevation at the bridge is 7540 and you are about 65 minutes into the ride.

10 mile mark: elevation 7570, 70 minutes into the ride. To your right you'll see the site of an old mine and maybe a small herd of goats. Further along is the Swiss Village Trailer Park on your right. About 1/10 mile south of the trailer park is a small suspension bridge over the river to your left which is a shortcut to the Ouray Hot Springs Pool. Continue on the road to a large trailer/camping park called 4J+1+1+1. At the south end of this park turn left, go two blocks to Main Street, Ouray. Your final elevation is 7740. Trip length about 80 minutes, distance 11.5 mile

8. ORVIS HOT SPRINGS

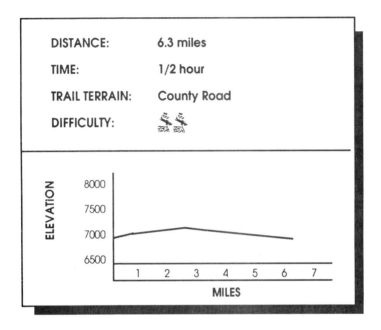

DISTANCE:	6.3 miles
TIME:	1/2 hour
TRAIL TERRAIN:	County Road
DIFFICULTY:	

ELEVATION

8000
7500
7000
6500

1 2 3 4 5 6 7

MILES

This is a small ride of 6.3 miles, about thirty minutes. •Follow the directions of the River Road ride to the intersection of County Road 23 and County Road 3A (the 3.2 mile mark, 18 minutes from Ridgway.) Instead of staying on Road 23 follow Road 3A over the bridge and immediately turn left on County Road 3 heading just west of due north. One-tenth of a mile on your left you will see my first residence in this area, circa. 1980. It has been sold and bought about four times in the last fifteen years and the selling prices give you an excellent short history of real estate values in the area.

4.1 mile mark: the greenhouses on your right have a full history. From broccoli farm to carnation factory to tropical fish store, this structure has created more dreams than a late-night onion sandwich. On your left, like a government ex-

Orvis Hot Springs.

periment of the 1950s, is the Amerigas propane storage yard.

Just a bit further on your left is Orvis Hot Springs, 4.2 mile mark. This is a great place to relax, winter or summer, indoors or out, with or without clothes.

4.3 mile mark: intersection of Highway 550 and County Road 3. You can take the highway back north (turn left) to Ridgway (3 miles back to the Park) or retrace your route on dirt roads. If you take the highway go to the intersection of Highways 62 and 550 (5.85 mile mark) and turn left to Ridgway Town Park.

> **LAZINESS IS**
>
> **NOTHING MORE**
>
> **THAN THE HABIT OF**
>
> **RESTING BEFORE YOU**
>
> **GET TIRED.**
>
> -JULES RENARD

9. IDLEWILD ESCAPE HATCH

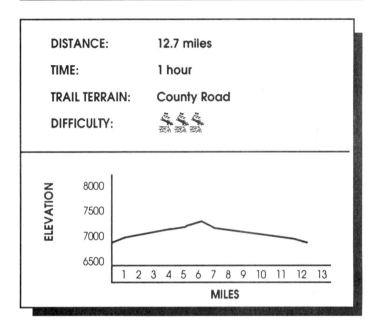

DISTANCE:	12.7 miles
TIME:	1 hour
TRAIL TERRAIN:	County Road
DIFFICULTY:	

•Follow the directions of the River Road ride to the intersection of County Road 17 and Suzanne Lane. Turn left, put your helmet on tight, and check your brakes. At the bottom of the hill the road turns right and then at an intersection you make a quick left off of Suzanne Lane onto Marguerite Drive which winds around and through Idlewild Estates to the Uncompahgre River. After passing a green metal building on your left, a woodworking shop, you will come to a stop sign. Turn left, north; you have returned to County Road 23, heading back toward the San Juan Guest Ranch. This road meanders through a beautiful stand of trees along the river. This part of the river has been the scene of controversy in the last few years because of the gravel extraction that is made so easy by the river's never ending attempt to wear down the San Juan Mountains. Pastures on your left, trees and river on your right. If you had turned right at the stop sign you

County Road 23 at Idlewild.

would have travelled to highway 550 and the local KOA Campground.

7.8 mile mark: the road turns left away from the river heading west back to the San Juan Guest Ranch. Back at the fork, the 8.5 mile mark, you continue back to Ridgway, retracing your tracks (4.2 miles back to Ridgway for a total of 12.7 miles) or taking the Orvis Ride.

> PESSIMIST:
>
> ONE WHO, WHEN HE
>
> HAS THE CHOICE OF
>
> TWO EVILS, CHOOSES
>
> BOTH.
>
> -OSCAR WILDE

IV. COW CREEK MAP

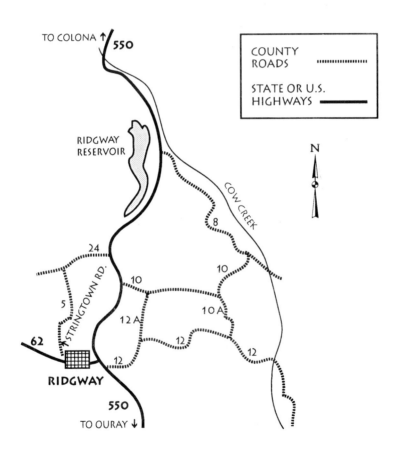

10. COW CREEK / BIG PINK

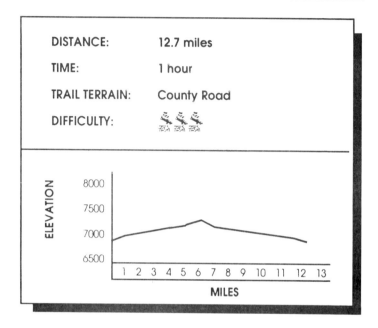

DISTANCE:	12.7 miles
TIME:	1 hour
TRAIL TERRAIN:	County Road
DIFFICULTY:	

ELEVATION

8000
7500
7000
6500

1 2 3 4 5 6 7 8 9 10 11 12 13

MILES

This ride takes you on a fairly level tour of the valley formed by Cow and Owl Creeks east and north of Ridgway. The trip is 11.5 miles with an elevation gain of only 360 feet. There are many offshoots from this trail so that you can ride all day if you wish. The ride is all on county roads and circles what I consider the loveliest inhabited lowlands in Ouray County. Trip time is approximately 75 minutes.

•Start at the Ridgway Town Park at an elevation of 6970. Head east on State Highway 62 to U.S. Highway 550. Turn right (south) on 550 and go 3/8 mile to County Road 12 where you turn left.

1.5 mile mark: elevation 7060; first a small white house then a large white house on your left as the road swings left and north.

The llamas of Big Pink.

2 mile mark: elevation 7060; it is 8:00 a.m. as I ride and write this description and three deer and a cottontail cross the road in front of me. At the 2.35 mile mark the road turns right.

2.5 mile mark: come to a "Y" in the road, you stay right on County Road 12. The left turn is County Road 12A. Elevation is 7100 as you go up a steep hill (two more bunnies).

2.85 mile mark: elevation 7190; 20 minutes into ride at the top of the hill.

3.2 mile mark: elevation 7170; OXO Ranch on your right, a large, working ranch which, hopefully, will not soon be replaced by 35 acre lots. Just passed two ranch workers repairing an irrigation ditch breech. At the 3.4 mile mark you pass the Walchle Guest House on the right.

3.6 mile mark: elevation 7170; road turns left at the entrances of OXO Ranch hands' houses.

4 mile mark: elevation 7170; road turns right and heads east. At the 4.3 mile mark you pass the Walchle Ranch on your left at an elevation of 7230. Continue up a steep rise.

4.5 mile mark: elevation 7300; you are at the top of a hill with good views of the Cimarrons, Chimney Peak and Courthouse Mountain to the east.

5 mile mark: elevation 7330; intersection with the road on your left being County Road 10A. Continuing straight on County Road 12 takes you on the Cow Creek ride which is described later. Turn left on 10A. Pass the Deerhawk Ranch on your left. Many birds out on the wires today, not to mention the ubiquitous deer. If you were to extrapolate the total deer population of the county from the number you see on the roads it would be astronomical.

> HAPPINESS IS NOT
>
> SOMETHING YOU
>
> EXPERIENCE IT IS
>
> SOMETHING YOU
>
> REMEMBER.
>
> -OSCAR LEVANT

5.5 mile mark: on your right are some bee hives as the road swings left.

6 mile mark: elevation 7330; high point of the ride, 42 minutes.

6.2 mile mark: you come to a stop sign at the intersection of county roads 10 and 10A. Turn left and head toward Highway 550. If you turn right you are on your way to Owl Creek Pass and/or the Ridgway Reservoir which are described later. As you head down you get an excellent view of the valley to your left. Bordering the road on the left is a large ranch that has changed hands three times in the last few years and is now owned by a media-mogul of the 1st-rank.

7 mile mark: elevation 7240; Just below Sneffels Mountain to the south is Elk Meadows, the sight of another ride described herein.

8 mile mark: elevation 7110; turn left here on County Road 12A. Continuing straight will bring you to highway 550 and a somewhat dangerous return to Ridgway on a state highway. You head east toward the entrance to the Double D Ranch, turning right and continuing on 12A. Off to the left you will see a large house that gives name to the Big Pink Ride. Head due south.

8.5 mile mark: elevation 7070; 55 minutes.

9 mile mark: elevation 7085; all downhill from here. Intersection looks familar, stay right and back on Road 12. Follow it back to Ridgway, past the red barn and the million birds-on-the-wire. Continue to Highway 550 or turn on the road immediately before the highway for a tour of the Super 8, Ridgway USA, and Trailtown. With either choice turn left at Highway 62 back to Ridgway Town Park, 11.5 miles from where you started. The True Grit is a good finishing point after a 75 minute ride.

ᘓᚼᗷ

11. Cow Creek

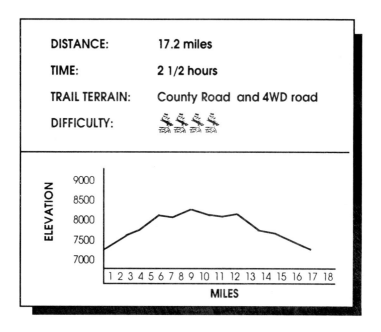

DISTANCE: 17.2 miles

TIME: 2 1/2 hours

TRAIL TERRAIN: County Road and 4WD road

DIFFICULTY:

ELEVATION
9000
8500
8000
7500
7000
1 2 3 4 5 6 7 8 9 10 11 12 13 14 15 16 17 18
MILES

This trip can be strenuous depending on your starting point. You may start in Ridgway, following the directions for the Big Pink/Cow Creek trip, riding five miles to the intersection of County Roads 12 and 10A. This is where we will begin our description. However, you can drive another 3.35 miles and park before crossing Cow Creek. You can drive across the creek only in a four-wheel drive vehicle and continue up a very steep hill for another two miles and park (the round trip from this point will only be about 8 miles and 85 minutes). Before crossing the creek a passenger vehicle is adequate. You should also be advised that the creek is impassable at certain times of the year (and day) because of the water level. There is a bridge, however, where you can carry your bike across the creek without getting wet.

Surveillance on the way to Cow Creek.

•Ride or drive the five miles to the intersection of County Roads 12 and 10A. Continue straight on Road 12, National Forest Access. Starting elevation 7340. Round trip of about 2 1/2 hours.

1 mile mark: elevation 7530; at the 1.2 mile mark there are two stock pens on the left as you start up a rise heading due east.

1.5 mile mark: elevation 7650; leaving the Ridgway Fire District, so if you spontaneously combust you're on your own.

1.65 mile mark: elevation 7680; top of the climb, heading down to Cow Creek. Cross a cattle guard at the 1.8 mile mark.

2.1 mile mark: elevation 7680; cross a second cattle guard, going downhill through private property so stay on the road.

2.15 mile mark: elevation 7520; Cow Creek is on your left as you parallel it heading for the creek crosssing. There are many campsites on both sides of the creek.

3.35 mile mark: elevation 7540; approximately 30 minutes into the ride the road crosses the creek. During the spring and early summer there probably is too much water to cross. Also at other times of the year the stream may be impassable later in the day because of melting. However, there is another crossing opportunity. Instead of following the road into the creek continue straight paralleling the stream as much as possible depending on the water level. Follow a rather indistinct path through river bed or over hills adjacent to river bed for 5 to 10 minutes walking time. As creek turns sharply right you will come upon a big water pipe with stairs and a walking platform attached by which you can cross the creek. Cross over, turn left and follow a road 1/4 mile to where you will intersect with the road that crossed the creek. You will know this is the correct road because there will be a sign (up about 1/10 mile from where road crosses creek) listing distances to certain trails and creeks: Courthouse Creek 1 mile; Red Creek 2 miles; Green Mountain Trail 5 miles; and Wetterhorn Basin 10 miles. You are on a narrow, winding, four-wheel dive road that is very steep.

> THE VERY PURPOSE OF
> OUR EXISTENCE IS TO
> RECONCILE THE
> GLOWING OPINION WE
> HOLD OF OURSELVES
> WITH THE APPALLING
> THINGS THAT OTHER
> PEOPLE THINK
> ABOUT US.
>
> - QUENTIN CRISP

4 mile mark: elevation 7780; road turns left as you start leveling out somewhat. Off to your right and south is a small gap through which cow creek flows. This road will go to the left of the gap. Cross a cattle guard at the 4.25 mile mark.

The gap at Cow Creek.

4.75 mile mark: elevation 8000; come upon a large number of moss covered rocks here and strangely enough the road is very rocky, with water making it extremely slippery.

4.85 mile mark: cross a cattle guard that marks the entrance to the National Forest; between 50 and 60 minutes to this point.

5 mile mark: elevation 8100; sign on your left says Courthouse Trail, Green Mountain Trail 2 miles, and West Fork 6 miles. Continue to top of hill for another parking area if you so choose. The road begins to fall.

5.5 mile mark: elevation 8010; road continues to descend to Cow Creek on your right which you should be able to hear.

6 mile mark: elevation 8030; the road has begun to rise and you cross a small tributary of Cow Creek coming down from your left. This is my favorite type of ride: ups and downs but overall level; a high heartbeat but no flapping tongues.

6.5 mile mark: elevation 8040; just passed an open

meadow with some newly downed trees.

7 mile mark: elevation 8070; come out of the trees right at Cow Creek. The road parallels the creek on your right. You can see by the width of the creek that this is quite the wash, quite the watershed. And then, about 90 minutes into the ride the road disappears into the creek and you must portage a small distance. I did this ride in the Fall so if you do it at another time be prepared for different stream conditions.

7.4 mile mark: elevation 8100; heading up hill above Cow Creek and then level off at 8220 feet.

8 mile mark: elevation 8260; 100 miutes. You don't want to get caught on this road when it rains. It turns to wheel-choking mud easily and can turn a pleasant ride into a long walk.

8.3 mile mark: elevation 8340; a small sign of to your left: Green Mountain Trail No. 219" heads off at a 45 degree angle from the road. A bit farther on you come to a fork, stay left. There are some nice campsites along the creek.

8.5 mile mark: elevation 8300; about 110 minutes brings you to a small washout of the road.

8.6 mile mark: elevation 8270; cross a small stream and the end of the road. Off to the left is the foot trail to Wetterhorn Basin while off to your right is an outhouse provided by your friendly National Forest. Return for a round trip of 2 to 2 1/2 hours.

⊗

12. COW CREEK / RIDGWAY RESERVOIR

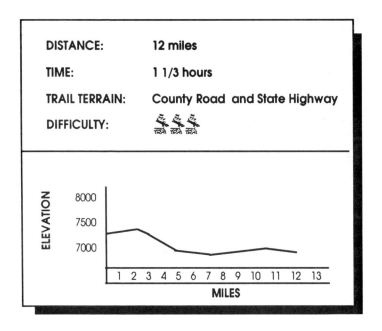

DISTANCE: **12 miles**

TIME: **1 1/3 hours**

TRAIL TERRAIN: **County Road and State Highway**

DIFFICULTY:

ELEVATION

8000
7500
7000

1 2 3 4 5 6 7 8 9 10 11 12 13
MILES

•The description of this ride begins east and north of Ridgway at the intersection of Ouray County Roads 10 and 10A. Follow the ride description for BIG PINK/COW CREEK to get to this intersection (6.2 miles from Ridgway) or consult the maps for a shorter drive. This ride begins at an elevation of 7350, circles around to the west, follows the Reservoir, and returns to Ridgway on String Town Road. It is mainly down hill all the way from the intersection, totaling 12 miles and taking 1 1/3 hours. To ride it this way would take a shuttle. It is a pretty ride but remember you must ride on the highway for a short distance (a large shoulder makes this less precarious). Consult your maps for different options on this ride. Follow road 10 north.

.2 mile mark: Cedar Hills Ranch is on your left.

Sleeping Indian Ranch house.

1.4 mile mark: elevation 7330; come to an intersection, turn left on County Road 8. You will follow this road until it intersects with State Highway 550.

1.5 mile mark: elevation 7330; passing through ranch and pasture land.

2 mile mark: elevation 7420; 15 minutes brings you to a "Blind Curve" sign. It is down hill to the highway from here.

2.5 mile mark: elevation 7330; pass the Broken Arrow Ranch on your left.

3 mile mark: elevation 7300; Cow Creek, Owl Creek, Lou Creek, and Nate Creek are on your right running through pasture land.

3.5 mile mark: elevation 7280.

4 mile mark: elevation 7150. Good down hill speed from here to highway.

4.5 mile mark: elevation 7050; after 28 minutes you'll pass a Sleeping Indian Ranch house on your right that is

Water skiing in December on the Reservoir.

known for it's beautiful, red Christmas lights.

4.9 mile mark: elevation 6980; intersection of County Road 8 and Highway 550. Turn left and go south toward the main entrance to Ridgway State Park. On your right you will see a swimming beach, boat dock, campground, and day use area. At the reservoir walkers and bikers are admitted free, vehicles are charged $4.

5 mile mark: elevation 6980; 32 minutes.

5.5 mile mark: elevation 6960.

6 mile mark: elevation 6990; here is the main entrance to the Ridgway State Recreation Area—Dutch Charlie Site. You may enter here and connect with the Uncompahgre Riverway Trail, page 95.

6.5 mile mark: elevation 6930; southeast edge of reservoir.

7 mile mark: elevation 6940; 42 minutes. You come to another entrance to the park called Dallas Creek Area. Turn right here off the highway and follow the road through the Entrance-Ticket Booth to the stop sign, turn left towards the Nature Area. Continue on road, pass the Deer Run Picnic Area, pass the kid's playground and bathrooms, if you can, to another parking area and bathroom complex. Leave the road here and take the sidewalk/bike path south to an exit on County Road 24.

8.5 mile mark: elevation 6940; 50 minutes. At the intersection of the path and County Road 24, turn right and continue on road 24 past two entrances to Dallas Meadows Subdivision (the second at the 9 mile mark, elevation 6990).

> EVERYBODY GETS SO MUCH MORE INFORMATION ALL DAY LONG THAT THEY LOSE THEIR COMMON SENSE.
>
> -GERTRUDE STEIN

9.4 mile mark: elevation 7000; turn left at the intersection and follow County Road 5 as it winds back to Ridgway.

10 mile mark: elevation 7070; 60 minutes.

11 mile mark: elevation 7050. Continue south on the road until the first stop sign at Amelia (County Road 5) and Charles Streets. Continue straight one more block to Clinton Street, turn left and go to the Town Park. The trip is 12 miles and takes about 80 minutes.

⬡

V. OWL CREEK MAP

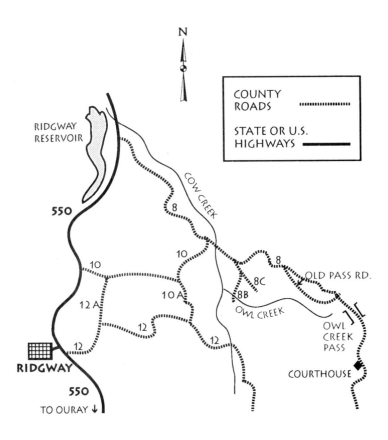

N

| COUNTY ROADS | ············· |
| STATE OR U.S. HIGHWAYS | ——— |

RIDGWAY RESERVOIR

550

COW CREEK

8

10

10

8

OLD PASS RD.

8C

8B

OWL CREEK

10 A

12 A

12

12

12

OWL CREEK PASS

RIDGWAY

COURTHOUSE

550

TO OURAY ↓

13. Owl Creek / Ranches

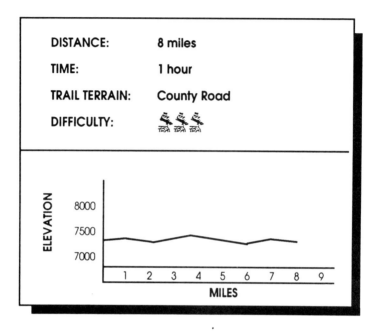

DISTANCE:	8 miles
TIME:	1 hour
TRAIL TERRAIN:	County Road
DIFFICULTY:	🚴 🚴 🚴

ELEVATION

8000
7500
7000

1 2 3 4 5 6 7 8 9

MILES

This ride takes you through some of the many ranches of the Owl Creek/Cow Creek valley. The round trip is about 8 miles from the intersection of County Roads 10 and 10A which is 6.2 miles from Ridgway (see directions For Big Pink/Cow Creek or your maps). From this ride you can also go up and over Owl Creek Pass to Courthouse Mountain for a long trip from Ridgway or any length ride in between.

•Begin at the intersection of County Roads 10 and 10A at an elevation of 7300. You can ride to this point or drive.

.2 mile mark: Cedar Hills Ranch on your left as you head north on road 10.

.5 mile mark: elevation 7310; at .7 mile mark, on your right, is a gate saying "No Trespassing" and a mail box. Off

The entrance Sleeping Indian Ranch.

the road at this point is a white building which used to be a school house for this area.

1 mile mark: elevation 7310; both sides of this road belong to the Wolf Ranch.

1.3 mile mark: you come to a "T" intersection, turn right on County Road 8 toward Owl Creek Pass.

1.5 mile mark: elevation 7280; on your left are some stock pens and the entrance to the Sleeping Indian Ranch.

1.8 mile mark: begin to descend to Cow Creek and pass the first of two entrances to the Cow Creek Community Hall, owned by the Ouray County Sheriff's Possee and the site of many wild parties and community celebrations.

2 mile mark: elevation 7240; parallelling Cow Creek on your left.

2.4 mile mark: crossing Cow Creek. Continue up the hill to a fork in the road.

2.85 mile mark: elevation 7350; take the right fork toward the J Bar M Ranch, the Chimney Peak Ranch, and the Owl Creek Ranch. This is a county road but both sides are

> GOD CREATED MAN
> AND, FINDING HIM NOT
> SUFFICIENTLY ALONE,
> GAVE HIM A
> COMPANION TO MAKE
> HIM FEEL HIS SOLITUDE
> MORE KEENLY.
>
> - PAUL VALERY

private property; please obey all signs. About .3 mile from the intersection you will pass the entrance to the Chimney Peak Ranch; at the .9 mile mark the J Bar M, and at the 1.2 mark you are at a dead end.

Return the way you came, to the intersection of roads 10 and 10A or when you hit Co. Rd. 8 turn right and go uphill toward Owl Creek Pass which is described next.

14. OWL CREEK / VISTA POINT

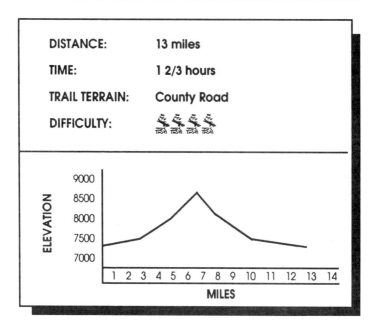

DISTANCE:	13 miles
TIME:	1 2/3 hours
TRAIL TERRAIN:	County Road
DIFFICULTY:	

•The description of this ride begins near the end of the Owl Creek/Ranch Ride at the 2.85 mile mark where you continue up the hill on County Road 8 instead of turning right to a dead end. Starting at the intersection of County Roads 10 and 10A follow the directions of the above ride. From this point, at an elevation fof 7350, it is about 3.5 miles uphill to Vista Point. The elevation gain is 1270. The distance from roads 10 and 10a is about 6.5 miles. This is a tough climb, physically if not technically. There are many fine views but they are attained by steep elevation gains. Round trip time from 10 and 10A is about 100 minutes.

   3 mile mark: elevation 7430; 21 minutes into the ride (ride description up to this point can be found in the preceeding description of the Owl Creek/Ranch Ride).

   3.2 mile mark: elevation 7460; National Forest Sign

Profile of a sleeping Indian.

stating distances: Owl Creek Pass 10 miles; Silver Jack Reservoir 18 miles; U.S. Highway 50 (running east and west from Montrose to Gunnison) 37 miles.

3.5 mile mark: elevation 7540; 26 minutes.

3.7 mile mark: elevation 7610; cattle guard.

4 mile mark: elevation 7680; 32 minutes.

4.1 mile mark: to the right is a small turnout as the road turns southeast from which you can see the the profile of the Sleeping Indian. Due south is Mt. Sneffels. To the left (east), foreground, is a green mountain to the left of which is the Indian head, seen as if he or she were laying on his or her back.

4.3 mile mark: elevation 7760; the road swings left by a metal gate with a sign stating "Road Closed." This is the old Owl Creek Road which was abandoned because it was subject to frequent closings from mudslides. The initial poprtion of this old road was an access road through private property and was returned to the owners when abandoned. Stay off of it.

4.5 mile mark: elevation 7890; 40 minutes.

5 mile mark: elevation 8090; 47 minutes.

5.4 mile mark: elevation 8240; 53 minutes. Cross a cattle guard and enter the world of the National Forest (Forest Road 858).

5.5 mile mark: elevation 8290; 56 minutes.

6 mile mark: elevation 8470; 63 minutes.

> ONE'S NEED FOR
> LONELINESS IS NOT
> SATISFIED IF ONE
> SITS AT A TABLE
> ALONE. THERE MUST
> BE EMPTY CHAIRS
> AS WELL.
>
> - KARL KRAUS

6.4 mile mark: elevation 8620; National Forest sign indicating Vista Point on your right. Vista Point is about .1 mile down the road on your right. Strangely enough it is a good place to view Courthouse Mountain and Chimney Peak. This is the end of this rides' description. You can return to your starting point or go on to the description of the Owl Creek/Old Road Ride which will take you from here further up Owl Creek Pass.

🚲

15. Owl Creek / Old Pass Road

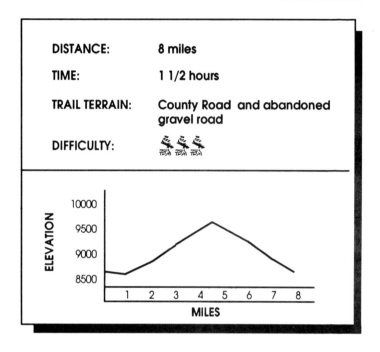

DISTANCE: 8 miles

TIME: 1 1/2 hours

TRAIL TERRAIN: County Road and abandoned gravel road

DIFFICULTY:

This is another section of the Owl Creek Pass road. It travels from Vista Point up the old Owl Creek Pass Road to the new road and back to Vista Point. The round trip is 8 miles and takes about 85 minutes. You can continue on up and over the pass if you wish. You can park at Vista Point or at any other point between Vista Point and Ridgway. Consult the map or other ride descriptions if you want to lengthen this ride. The elevation gain from Vista point is only 930 feet in approximately 4.5 miles, so it is somewhat strenuous but not as taxing as the ride up to Vista Point. I find it very pleasing because it is on a closed road with no other traffic. There are also many side roads and trails that can turn this small ride into an all day experience.

•For directions to this point see ride description for Owl

Courthouse Mountain.

Creek/Vista Point. At the turn that takes you .1 mile back to the Vista Point parking area you will see 4 boulders blocking a road to large vehicles. Follow this path/road downhill. It looks like an ATV track because it is; hunters also use it.

.1 mile mark: cross some aspen logs that make a watery bogg passable.

.5 mile mark: elevation 8410; you meet the old road, to the right it passes through private property and will hook-

Chimney Peak.

up with the new road. This road is closed to regular vehicles, but squirrels and birds are plentiful. Turn left and head up hill.

1 mile mark: elevation 8560; 15 minutes. You just passed one of the slide areas that made this road difficult to keep open for passenger vehicles. There are many side roads off this track that were and/or are used for logging, hunting, fishing, hiking, firweood cutting, etc. This is National Forest so feel free to explore.

1.5 mile mark: elevation 8710; 22 minutes. As you pass through a double gate you get a good view of Courthouse Mountain and Chimney Peak just south of east. They're getting closer.

2 mile mark: elevation 8870; 30 minutes.

2.4 mile mark: elevation 9010; another slide area.

2.5 mile mark: elevation 9040; at the 2.6 mile mark you pass through another slough area.

3 mile mark: elevation 9190; 46 minutes. What a nice ride this is.

3.5 mile mark: elevation 9320; 53 minutes. Pulse at a nice seady 130 per minute. Just past the 3.6 mile mark you come to 10 large boulders in the middle of the road. Continue through this blockage to the intersection with the new Owl Creek Pass Road. If you turn right here you will continue up to the top of the pass. For this ride, however, we will turn left and follow the new road back to Vista Point.

> PEOPLE DEMAND FREEDOM OF SPEECH TO MAKE UP FOR THE FREEDOM OF THOUHT WHICH THEY AVOID.
>
> -KIERKEGAARD

3.7 mile mark: elevation 9380; 57 minutes. Turn left going up hill for a ways before we start the long down hill to Vista Point.

4 mile mark: elevation 9450; 61 minutes.

4.5 mile mark: elevation 9550; 67 minutes. Just crossed a cattle guard.

5 mile mark: elevation 9490; 70 minutes.

6 mile mark: elevation 9270; 76 minutes.

7 mile mark: elevation 8950; 80 minutes.

7.6 mile mark: come to a road leading off to the left which is a short dead-end. Pass it.

8 mile mark: back to Vista Point after 86 minutes.

16. Owl Creek Pass

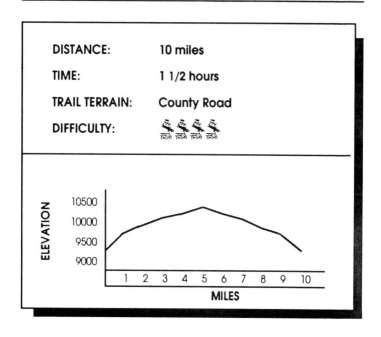

DISTANCE: 10 miles

TIME: 1 1/2 hours

TRAIL TERRAIN: County Road

DIFFICULTY:

ELEVATION

10500
10000
9500
9000

1 2 3 4 5 6 7 8 9 10

MILES

•This is the final ride in the Owl Creek series. You can begin it at the intersection of the old and new roads which is 4.3 miles above Vista Point on the new road or 3.7 miles on the old road or from Vista Point or from Ridgway if you wish. From the intersection the round trip is 10 miles and takes about 85 minutes. The elevation gain is 1030 feet. Because of the altitude gain and the starting elevation I give this ride a 4 Pedal rating, but when doing it, especially if you start at the intersection and not farther below, it seemed more in the realm of a 3 Pedal rating. It is a beautiful ride, especally over the top, in the valley formed by the Cimarron Range on the east and Courthouse Mountain on the west Starting elevation is 9380.

.5 mile mark: elevation 9540.

1 mile mark: elevation 9680.

Forestry sign at Owl Creek Pass.

1.5 mile mark: elevation 9810; 20 minutes.

1.9 mile mark: elevation 9900; pass an open area on your left (at upper end you will see a sign reading "Nate Creek Ditch") that provides a good camping area and was the sight of many Bon Ton Restaurant staff parties during the early 1980s.

2 mile mark: elevation 9920; 24 minutes. Just passing a sign that looks back and indicates Chimney Peak and Courthouse Mountain (line up Chimney Peak and the sign and you will be looking almost due south).

2.5 mile mark: elevation 10040; 31 minutes.

2.6 mile mark: elevation 10080; cross a cattle guard and

The Cimarrons.

Courthouse Mountain.

pass through a double gate with sluice boxes on your right. You are at the summit with a sign reading 10140. Continue over the pass to the West Fork of the Cimarrons.

3 mile mark: elevation 10060; 35 minutes. You are at a fork in the road. Continuing straight will take you to Silver Jack reservoir and U.S. Highway 50 so turn right and head along the West Fork of the Cimarrons. This road is east of Courthouse Mountain and Chimney Peak heading south. This valley is very beautiful, especially during a summer sunset when you can get an alpenglow on the Cimarron Range and Pinnacles to the east.

> NINETY PERCENT OF
> THE POLITICIANS
> GIVE THE OTHER TEN
> PERCENT A
> BAD NAME.
>
> -HENRY KISSINGER

4 mile mark: elevation 10180; 43 minutes. There are many camping areas and side roads in this basin.

4.4 mile mark: road opens up to give good view of the entire valley.

4.5 mile mark: elevation 10280; 52 minutes.

4.6 mile mark: The beginning of the Courthouse Trail appears on your right as you enter more trees after passing through an open area. This trail is closed to all motorized vehicles and bicycles (Big Blue Wilderness).

5 mile mark: elevation 10410; 60 minutes. A sign stating "Narrow Very Rough Road" marks the end of our description. The road continues for a mile or so as a four-wheel drive road only; up to this point the road was able to be driven by a regular vehicle.

🚲

VI. DEXTER CREEK MAP

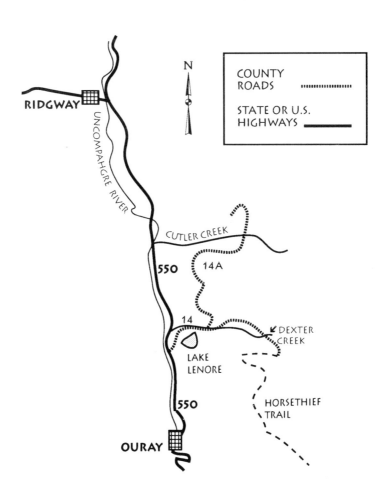

17. LAKE LENORE

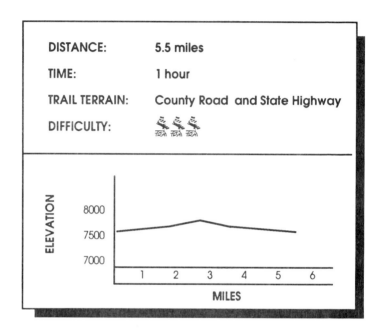

DISTANCE:	5.5 miles
TIME:	1 hour
TRAIL TERRAIN:	County Road and State Highway
DIFFICULTY:	

This is a short ride of only 5.5 miles rounnd trip. But you can use this as the beginning of two other rides, one of which is rated 5 Pedals in difficulty. From this ride, on state highway and county road, you get good views of Ouray and the Uncompahgre Valley along with a fairly good workout for the distance involved. Round trip time is about 60 minutes.

• Begin at the Ouray Hot Springs Pool at an elevation of 7620. Head north on Highway 550 out of town.

1 mile mark: pass the Daisy Inn der Ground on your right.

1.3 mile mark: Rotary Park on your right. Pass a highway sign on your right advertising the Bachelor Syracuse Mine and turn right at the road.

Lake Lenore.

1.7 mile mark: elevation 7630; this is your turn, as indicated by signs "Dexter Creek Road" and "Uncompahgre National Forest". Go uphill. At the 1.9 mile mark stay right when you see a sign on the left indicating Pine View.

> IT TAKES A
> WONDERFUL BRAIN
> AND EXQUISITE SENSES
> TO PRODUCE A FEW
> STUPID IDEAS.
>
> -SANTAYANA

2 mile mark: elevation 7700; sign on left says Panoramic Heights (known to some as Uranium Acres).

2.4 mile mark: pass a sign stating "Lake Lenore Game Refuge" indicating a profound belief in the sanctity of private property.

2.5 mile mark: elevation 7740.

2.7 mile mark: you have arrived at Lake Lenore but remember it is all private property. You can return to Ouray or follow the directions for Horsethief Trail or Cutler Creek which are coming right up.

18. Cutler Creek

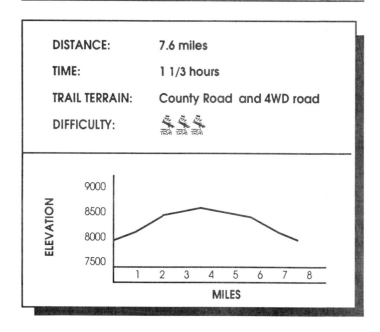

DISTANCE:	7.6 miles
TIME:	1 1/3 hours
TRAIL TERRAIN:	County Road and 4WD road
DIFFICULTY:	

•This ride begins just beyond Lake Lenore at the intersection of County Roads 14 and 14A. From this point the round trip is only 7.6 miles with an elevation gain of of 700 feet. If you ride from Ouray add another 5.5 miles and 120 feet. The majority of the ride is on improved dirt road and parallels the Uncompahgre Valley before turning east for a short incursion into the National Forest. The ride intersects the Cutler Creek Trailhead and the Baldy Trailhead. Cross the bridge at the intersection, taking County Road 14A, Cutler Creek Road, at an elevation of 7930.

.6 mile mark: elevation 8150; a panoramic view of the valley.

Dexter Creek.

1 mile mark: elevation 8170; entering Uncompahgre National Forest.

1.15 mile mark: elevation 8250; tailings on the hillside to your right with hill climbing at its best (or worst) with spectacular views.

1.5 mile mark: elevation 8520; top out at a fork in the road. The right road goes up into the forest, take the left road that parallels Cutler Creek.

2 mile mark: fork in the road with paths to left and right, stay centered.

2.3 mile mark: elevation 8450.

2.6 mile mark: a large open area to your right, as the road passes through a fence, is a staging/camping area for hunters. Stay left and go quickly and steeply down a hill to cross Cutler Creek. Just over the creek see a sign "Cutler Creek Trailhead." Continue on road.

2.8 mile mark: elevation 8470; your are north of Cutler Creek.

> IF THE WORLD SHOULD
> BLOW ITSELF UP, THE
> LAST AUDIBLE VOICE
> WOULD BE THAT OF AN
> EXPERT SAYING IT CAN'T
> BE DONE.
>
> - PETER USTINOV

3.4 mile mark: elevation 8590; you come to Baldy Trailhead which is closed to bikers like you. Continue on the road to your left. 3.4 mile mark: elevation 8590; you are on the north side of Cutler Creek looking across the ravine to the road which brought you in.

3.8 mile mark: elevation 8520; the road abruptly ends and you must return.

19. HORSETHIEF TRAIL

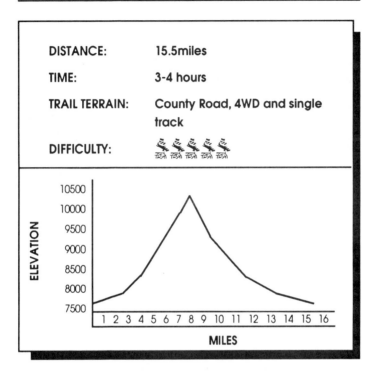

DISTANCE:	15.5miles
TIME:	3-4 hours
TRAIL TERRAIN:	County Road, 4WD and single track
DIFFICULTY:	

This is a 5 Pedal rated ride from wherever you begin: Ouray, Lake Lenore, or the beginning of the single track at the end of a four-wheel drive road. It is well worth the effort, however. From Ouray the elevation gain is over 2700 feet; the last two miles of the ride, which is a single track, rises over a 1000 feet. The round trip from Ouray is 15.5 miles. Time involved is from 3 to 4 hours. Read the description carefully and choose the starting point most approprate to your condition and ability. It's a lot of fun. Follow the directions to the end of the Lake Lenore ride; we will pick up the narrative from that point. Continue from Lake Lenore on Road 14 until you reach an intersection with Cutler Creek Road (County Road 14A); con-

Looking at Ouray from the top of Horsethief.

tinue on Road 14 to your right.

3 mile mark: elevation 7880; you level out and pass on your right the entrance to the Bachelor Syracuse Mine Tour. Just beyond the mine you enter the Uncompahgre National Forest.

3.5 mile mark: elevation 8040; the road continues to be passable by regular auto as it parallels Dexter Creek and crosses a small bridge at the 3.65 mile mark.

4 mile mark: elevation 8220; steep hill.

4.5 mile mark: elevation 8520; the road crosses the creek and becomes a four-wheel drive road. Just before the bridge is an area that looks like an old mine site, with the obligatory tailings piles. A sign by the bridge proclaims "Dexter Creek Trailhead." Follow the road up.

4.7 mile mark: elevation 8620; come to a fork in the road, stay to the right (there may be a sign saying "Horsethief Trail and Bridge to Heaven").

5 mile mark: elevation 8730; pass a small mileage sign indicating "3."

5.5 mile mark: elevation 9020; you are at the top of a rise. The road levels out as you pass a stock pen on your left and come to a fork: stay right as the left path dead ends among some tailings piles. Road continues uphill and divides around two trees.

5.85 mile mark: elevation 9270; road comes to a sign that says Horse Thief Trail #215, Bridge of Heaven 4 miles, Difficulty Creek 7 miles, American Flats 9.5 miles, and Engineer Mountain 11 miles (just up the road is a parking area). Follow the trail,which is an access to the summer range of the area's Big Horn Sheep population. The trail switches back on itself numerous times as we gain elevation quickly. Be aware that the trail is a single track used by horses, pack trips, and hikers so be prepared for surprises and always give way. From this point to where we stop is a little less than two miles. Since this is an alternate parking area we will begin a new mileage count from this point.

.2 mile mark: elevation 9390.

.3 mile mark: elevation 9430.

.4 mile mark: elevation 9480.

.5 mile mark: elevation 9530; as you can see, and feel, the elevation gain is quick. Just before the .7 mile mark the trail turns left and another trail goes off to the right. There is a nice view on this right trail but your destination lies to the left.

Weathering tree atop Horsethief.

.7 mile mark: elevation 9650; 19 minutes from beginning of single track.

1 mile mark: elevation 9800; 25 minutes. Be aware of tree roots on this track, the major obstacles. You will begin a series of switchbacks and at the 1.25 mile mark you will pass a clearing to your right as you steeply climb and turn left back into the trees.

1.4 mile mark: elevation 10030; 36 minutes. The trail is parallel to a small ravine (the open area we saw two switch backs.) A large root crosses the trail here. You will come to a fork, stay to the left (main trail). Right after the fork look back north to get a good view of the Uncompahgre Valley; at times you can even see the La Sal Mountains of east-central Utah by looking west over Black Lake.

> **IF YOU CANNOT GET RID OF THE FAMILY SKELETON, YOU MAY AS WELL MAKE IT DANCE.**
>
> - GEORGE BERNARD SHAW

1.5 mile mark: elevation 10090; 41 minutes.

1.7 mile mark: elevation 10210; 46 minutes, pulse 150.

1.8 mile mark: elevation 10270; take the left path at a fork. Either way gets you to the same place but going right entails walking and pushing.

1.9 mile mark: elevation 10340; 52 minutes. You are at the top. There is a sign pointing back the way you came stating "Horse Thief Trail #215, Wedge Mine 1.5 miles, Dexter Creek 3 miles. "The path continues to the left as "Horse Thief Trail" to "Bridge of Heaven 2.5 miles, Difficulty Creek 5.5 miles, American Flats 8 miles, and Engineer Mountain 9.5 miles." Continue if you like, steeper and higher, I've had enough. To your right, walking out on the rocks, great views of Ouray, the valley, Yankee Boy Basin, Mt. Abrahms, the Million Dollar Highway and the San Juans. About 20 minutes to get back down the single track.

🚲

VII. ELK MEADOWS MAP

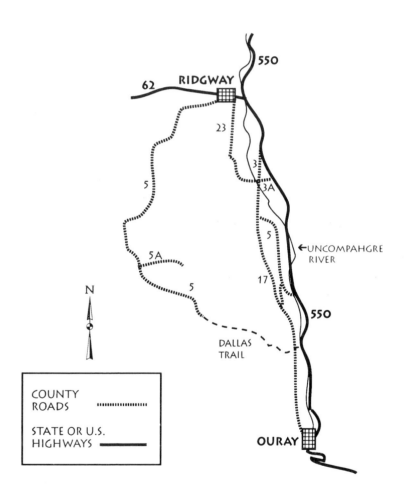

20. ELK MEADOWS/NAT'L FOREST ACCESS

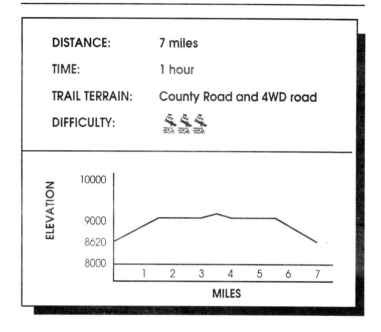

DISTANCE:	7 miles
TIME:	1 hour
TRAIL TERRAIN:	County Road and 4WD road
DIFFICULTY:	

This is a lovely ride on a four-wheel drive through private property and National Forest. Beginning at an elevation of 8620 you can ride to the top of the pass which is 6 miles away at an elevation of 10010. The climb really begins at the 3.5 mile mark, so you can enjoy the scenery without going all out. I recommend this ride highly because of the beauty and seclusion, and especially for the colors in the fall. The rating of this ride can be one pedal or five, depending on where you start, and finish. This is the start of the Dallas Trail Ride which is a single track and rates 5 Pedals in difficulty. Round trip on this first section is a little over 7 miles and one hour.

•Start in Ridgway at the Town Park at an elevation of 6970. We will drive six miles on a county road to a parking area. To increase your workout you can ride this stretch.

Parking area at Elk Meadows trailhead.

Go south on Lena Street 2 blocks to Moffat Street, turn right and go 5 blocks to Amelia Street. Turn left, head south for .25 mile, cross a small creek (Cottonwood Creek), and turn right on Ouray County Road 5. Follow this road for six miles until you reach the top (you"ll know when you see it) at an intersection where the road forks: one road going south over a cattle guard, the other turning left and east and entering the Elk Meadows Subdivision. You will take the right fork and take this access road to the Uncompahgre National Forest. (You may park here or travel the road another 1.5 mile to the top of a ridge to reduce your climb). The drive from Ridgway and to the National Forest border is passable to passenger cars, weather permitting. We will begin our description from this intersection at the Elk Meadows Subdivision turn.

Beginning at the cattle guard, elevation 8620, at the intersection of the National Forest Access Road, County Road 5, and County Road 5A (the road to the east to Elk Meadows Subdivision) continue south on the access road. The first 4 or 5 miles on this road is on private property owned by the late Waylon Philips who also owned the historic Beaumont Hotel in Ouray. Stay on the road until you reach the National Forest boundary, which is clearly marked. Follow the road as it climbs to a ridge overlooking the Sneffels Range.

1 mile mark: as you come out of the trees a large meadow spreads out before you. Continue to climb toward the ridge line.

1.55 mile mark: elevation 9090; this is the top of the ridge. You will see a small mileage sign saying "9." This is also a parking area if you want to avoid the initial climb. Follow the road as it drops away from the ridge; a good place to test your brakes.

2.55 mile mark: elevation 9050; mileage post "10."

3 mile mark: elevation 9090; following an irrigation creek on your right. You come to a fork in the road. Continue to your left; the right trail over the creek is an access road to head waters of the Town of Ridgway water supply.

> NEVER FEEL
>
> REMORSE FOR
>
> WHAT YOU HAVE
>
> THOUGHT ABOUT
>
> YOUR WIFE. SHE
>
> HAS THOUGHT
>
> MUCH WORSE
>
> THINGS ABOUT
>
> YOU.
>
> - JEAN ROSTAND

3.55 mile mark: elevation 9170; on your right is the Bear Creek Forest and Wildlife Retreat. Continue down hill, turn left, cross a cattle guard marking the entrance to the Uncompahgre National Forest. The road begins to climb

The Sneffels Range.

at this point and will intersect the Dallas Trail at its top. It is also the beginning of a radical change in the effort needed to ride so we will begin a new trail description or you can return the way you came. Round trip for this section is about an hour.

21. ELK MEADOWS/DALLAS TRAIL

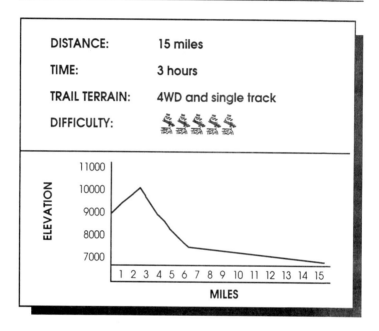

DISTANCE:	15 miles
TIME:	3 hours
TRAIL TERRAIN:	4WD and single track
DIFFICULTY:	

We begin the description at the boundary of the Uncompahgre National Forest and the Elk Meadows access road (see the preceeding description, National Forest/Elk Meadows Access). This road continues to the top of the pass and turns into a single track for the ride down. From an elevation of 9150 to the top elevation of 10010 takes only 2.25 miles. The single track on the down side is steep and technically difficult; make sure your bike, especially your brakes, is ready for this ride.

•Beginning at the cattle guard follow the road as it almost immediately forks. The left fork is a deadend, stay right. Put it in low gear as we start climbing.

.35 mile mark: elevation 9300; climbing now, breathing hard, be patient, take it slow, we got a long way to go.

.55 mile mark: the road swings left at a camp site favored

On the way to the Dallas Trail.

by deer and elk hunters-maybe that's why its called Elk Meadows. Now that you are in the National Forest feel free to investigate the many trails and roads that criss-cross the area.

.7 mile mark: you cross a relatively large dry creek bed, Coal Creek.

.85 mile mark: elevation 9410; about 15 minutes. You come to an open meadow with some sort of measuring station off to your left. Continue up a steeper than normal hill.

1.1 mile mark: elevation 9550; come to a fork, stay right.

1.6 mile mark: elevation 9670; 26 minutes. Come to an open meadow as the road turns left and heads almost due east. Looking up the road you can see it as it again enters the trees. To the left of this entrance you can see a small saddle that marks the top of the pass. As you ride through this open area, at about the middle, turn and look back north to see the Grand Mesa, to the left of which is Grand Junction. In the foreground is Log Hill Mesa.

1.85 miles: elevation 9780; come to a "Y" in the road, stay

The eastern end of the Sneffels Range.

to the left as the road goes through 2 evergreens, over some small streams, and then up a hill that seems to slope away to your left at a 30 degree angle. Don't always follow your inclinations. Almost to the top.

2 mile mark: elevation 9830; 35 minutes. It looks like the top but it isn't. You head down hill. Doesn't that feel good, using your brakes. Almost immediately you'll see a tree, growing, in the middle of the road. Say hello and continue on the road as it swings right and comes to a "Y."The road to the left is a four-wheel drive track that eventually deadends at a locked gate, private property and fences. Take the path to the right that quickly turns into a single track as we resume our climb to the real top. The path parallels a fallen tree-filled meadow to the left.

2.25 mile mark: elevation 9870; come out of the trees to the upper (southeast) end of a meadow named the Burn. Almost there.

2.35 mile mark: elevation 10,010; 45 minutes. The top. Come to a gate that says "Forest Service, Department of Agriculture-Please Close Gate". Open the gate, go through the gate, close the gate, you are one with your government.

This is a good place to rest, eat, check your brakes, and/or take a few gulps of oxygen. Follow the single track along the left side of the meadow (north side). This can be a dangerous descent if you are not careful and aware. Check to make sure your helmet is on and brain is working. Watch for rocks, tree roots, loose dirt and drop-offs.

2.55 mile mark: as you near the end of the meadow the trail will seem to disappear. Keep your head. At a 4" X 4" post sticking out of the ground make a 180 degree turn to your right and traverse back down the hill (almost due south) toward another post about a 100 yards away. You'll pick up a destinct trail again at that post. Follow the trail out of the meadow, through a field of skunk cabbage and back into the forest.

> EXISTENTIALISM
> MEANS THAT NO
> ONE ELSE CAN TAKE
> A BATH FOR YOU.
>
> -DELMORE SCHWARTZ

2.65 mile mark: elevation 9970; this trail can get extremely slippery from rain, snow or horses, so be careful.

2.85 mile mark: elevation 9650; a wooden bridge crosses a small creek.

3.15 mile mark: elevation 9580; you are in a area of many downed trees where you must walk or be a good jumper. It's fun going downhil, through some switchbacks. Keep those wheels moving and brake sparingly because when those wheels aren't spinning you have a tendency to fall over.

3.85 mile mark: elevation 9080; after a sharp switchback over a small creek you come to a fork-stay left downhill following a sign stating "Dallas Trail".

3.95 mile mark: elevation 9000; a swampy area where you must carry your bike through some water in order to keep those all-important brakes dry.

4.05 mile mark: heavily rutted switch back brings a surprise as you round a corner and encounter a newly felled tree across the track.

4.35 mile mark: elevation 8650; 90 minutes.

4.65 mile mark: elevation 8440; you encounter an old, abandoned building on your left.

4.85 mile mark: elevation 8390; come to a "Y", go left downhill.

5.15 mile mark: elevation 8160; 105 minutes. As you break out of the trees you can see Dexter Creek and what I call Uranium Acres across the valley and up the other side. Down by the river is the Ouray sewer plant.

5.45 mile mark: elevation 7970; 110 minutes. Come to yet another "Y", stay to left on Dallas Trail which brings you to another "Y" where you again stay left.

5.65 mile mark: rock outcropping.

5.85 mile mark: elevation 7910; you are at an overlook. As you continue down you encounter very steep, narrow and hairy inclines; very walkable switchbacks.

6.25 mile mark: red rock outcropping. Come to a fork. You will have a tendency to follow switchback to your right but don't do it, go left instead.

6.35 mile mark: elevation 7570; about 2 hours. You intersect with County Road 23. To your right is Ouray; to the left is Ridgway. You must make-up your own mind which is the road less travelled, not to mention where you are parked. It is 8.7 miles to Ridgway on this road (see the description for the River Road Ride).

⚲

VIII. Additional Rides

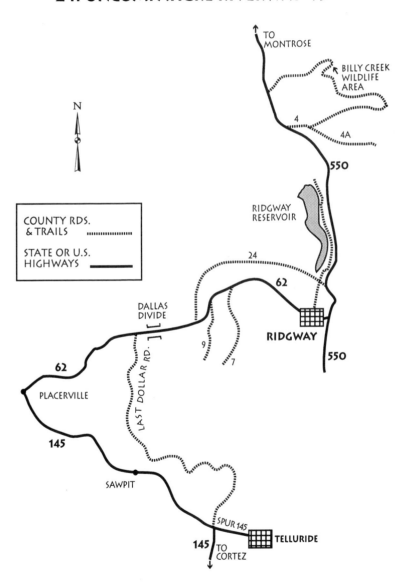

22. BILLY CREEK

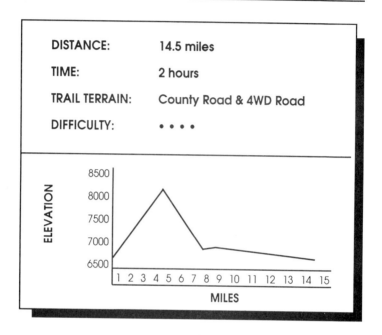

DISTANCE:	14.5 miles
TIME:	2 hours
TRAIL TERRAIN:	County Road & 4WD Road
DIFFICULTY:	• • • •

This is one of many possible rides through the Billy Creek State Wildlife Area north of Ridgway. There is an elevation gain of 1400 feet in the first 4.5 miles so this ride is rated four pedals. The ride begins 8 miles north of Ridgway and runs on county roads for 14.5 miles. They are very lightly traveled except for many birds.

Beginning from the Ridgway Town Park, turn east on State Highway 62 to Highway 550 where you turn north, heading toward Montrose. At the 8 mile mark you pass the northern entrance to the Ridgway State Park. Almost a mile farther north is County Road 4, Silverado Estates. Park about 1/4 mile before this right hand turn on an old highway. Start here at an elevation of 6680 feet.

.9 mile mark: stay left as you come to a "Y."

Birds of Billy Creek.

1.15 mile mark: cross a cattle guard that is a boundary for state land beyond.

1.5 mile mark: "Welcome to Your State Wildlife Area — Billy Creek." Another "Y" in the road; go left. To the right is County Road 4A. Elevation is 7010 feet, fifteen minutes into the ride.

2 mile mark: looking to the southeast, in the foreground is Enchanted Mesa (on the east side of the reservoir) with Mt. Sneffels in the background. Elevation is 7180.

> A PATRIOT MUST
>
> ALWAYS BE READY
>
> TO DEFEND HIS
>
> COUNTRY AGAINST
>
> HIS GOVERNMENT.
>
> - EDWARD ABBEY

2.5 mile mark: at an elevation of 7410 you cross a cattle guard with a sign reading "Private Land Here to Next Cattle Guard."

3 mile mark: elevation 7580; approximately 40 minutes.

4 mile mark: elevation 7950; 55 minutes.

4.5 mile mark: you are at the top at an elevation of 8130 after a little over an hour of climbing. You are on the edge of a steep valley where, if you are as lucky as I was, you'll see four hawks dive-bombing some fantasy prey.

4.7 mile mark: at an elevation of 8150, you come to a "T" intersection, go left.

5.5 mile mark: at a cattle guard, elevation 7830. Once again, you cross a state land boundary.

6 mile mark: elevation is 7580. You are on a road where high speeds can be obtained, but switchbacks and washboard conditions advise caution.

7 mile mark: elevation 720; still descending.

7.9 mile mark: elevation 6850 — almost to the bottom, up a little hill and then down to Billy Creek. Many birds, including eagles, gather in this area during the fall nesting season.

8.4 mile mark: elevation 6970; approximately 90 minutes into ride as you crest a hill and pass a campground on the left (Alder Creek).

9.5 mile mark: cross Billy Creek. Continue to the 9.6 mile mark where you turn left at a "T," heading back to 550.

11.2 mile mark: cattle guard marks boundary of the Billy Creek State Wildlife Area. Turn left and follow the highway back to our starting point for a total of 14.4 miles in about 2 hours.

23. LAST DOLLAR

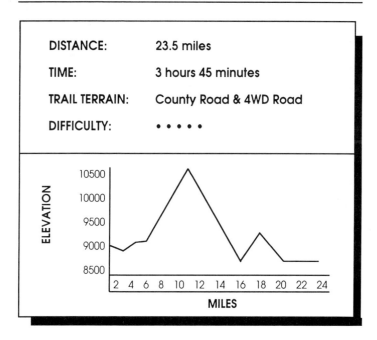

DISTANCE:	23.5 miles
TIME:	3 hours 45 minutes
TRAIL TERRAIN:	County Road & 4WD Road
DIFFICULTY:	• • • • •

With an elevation gain of almost 1600 feet, a distance of 23.5 miles, and a travel time of four hours; a five pedal designation does not seem inappropriate. However, this ride is mainly on county roads, with a portion on four-wheel drive tracts, and although long is not particularly difficult. It offers many beautiful vistas, from Utah to the Ingram Falls of Telluride. This is usually taken as a one-way trip with a car at each end.

Beginning at the Town Park in Ridgway go west out of town on State Highway 62 to the top of Dallas DIvide, 11 miles; elevation 8910. Continue west from the summit, 1.6 miles, where you will turn left on Last Dollar Road, National Forest Access. Go 1.3 more miles, park on the south side of the road at the top of a small rise that brings you to a mesa. You are at the 13.5 mile mark from Ridgway at an

The Peaks hotel to the right, town of Telluride at center.

elevation of 9010. Head southwest on the Last Dollar Road.

1 mile mark: elevation 9060; as you descend a hill at the bottom of which is an entrance to San Juan Vista.

2.5 mile mark: elevation 9090; you come to two wooden gates, one of which says "The Heath Ranch." Cross a cattle and continue crossing Hastings Mesa, the site of many interesting homes that do without the many advantages that power poles bring.

3 mile mark: elevation 8980; views of Lone Cone, Little Cone and the La Sals to the west, and the Wilson Peaks to the south.

3.9 mile mark: elevation 9070; 30 minutes. Take Last Dollar Road to your left at this intersection; to the right is the road to Sawpit, 7 miles distant.

4.5 mile mark: elevation 9140; below and to your right is the Sawpit Road; you are in the Big Park Pasture of the Heath Ranch.

4.8 mile mark: another entrance to the Howard and Ruth Heath Ranch.

5.4 mile mark: crossing Alder Creek; all uphill from here.

6 mile mark: elevation 9140; 52 minutes. Be sure you carry some bug spray — at these speeds they are just as fast as uphill bikers.

7.5 mile mark: elevation 9750; cross a cattle guard.

7.9 mile mark: cross a small creek with a little soaking pond off to the left.

8 mile mark: elevation 10000; 90 minutes; break out of the trees along a rail fence.

> PROGRESS
>
> WAS ALL RIGHT.
>
> ONLY IT WENT ON
>
> TOO LONG.
>
> - JAMES THURBER

8.3 mile mark: elevation 10120; a finger of land moves off the road to your right from which there are sites too numerous to list.

9 mile mark: elevation 10350; almost two hours. It is 3/4 of a mile to the top.

9.75 mile mark: elevation 10570. After two-plus hours you are at the top where there is a sign stating "Alder Creek No. 510, Whipple Mtn. Trail No. 419." Why do they call this a National Forest Access Road? The only access is at the very top where they can't sell any property. But it's still early. Adjust your helmut and head down — plenty of rocks, ruts and soft dirt so beware. Gloves are handy here.

11.5 mile mark: elevation 9780 with a rock field to your left.

12.5 mile mark: elevation 9500.

14.7 mile mark: elevation 8960; 2 hours, 33 minutes. Going down a hill toward a creek crossing so that you can go uphill again so that you can go down again — this ain't Kansas.

15.5 mile mark: elevation 8750; passing the Aldasoro Brothers "Sheepmen Build the Land" in plastic.

16 mile mark: elevation 8690; 2 hours 40 minutes. Stay left, last climb before Telluride.

16.3 mile mark: cross Sheep Creek, sign stating "Deep Creek Trail, Mill Creek 6 miles."

17.5 mile mark: elevation 9100; 3 hours.

18 mile mark: elevation 9080; just past the airport amidst the land of trophy homes.

18.5 mile mark: elevation 9110; beginning of the macadam road that doesn't stop until Telluride.

20.4 mile mark: turn left at this intersection and follow highway spur 45 to Telluride, elevation 8660.

23.5 mile mark: end of the road, 3 hours, 45 minutes.

🚲

21. THE UNCOMPAHGRE RIVERWAY

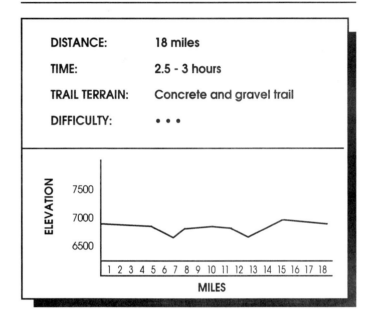

DISTANCE:	18 miles
TIME:	2.5 - 3 hours
TRAIL TERRAIN:	Concrete and gravel trail
DIFFICULTY:	• • •

The Uncompahgre Riverway project began in the late 1980s with the goal of establishing a bike trail from Delta to Ouray. A major section, completed in the summer of 2001, runs from Ridgway Town Park to the Ridgway Reservoir. It is a very beautiful ride, with only a few strenuous sections, that takes you along the Uncompahgre River and the eastern edge of the 1000 acre reservoir. All recreation sites in the park have bicycle access on approximately 15 miles of developed trails. Ridgway State Park offers exceptional views of the San Juans to the south, the Cimarron Range to the east and the Uncompahgre Plateau to the west.

•Start at the gazebo in Ridgway Town Park at an elevation of 6970. Go north on the concrete trail out of town, pass the town shop, wooden fence and sewer ponds, then San Miguel Power yard on the left as you parallel the Uncompahgre River. This complex is known as Fort Ridgway because of its unique western aspect.

.5 mile mark: cross old railroad trestle/bridge, you are now on the east side of the river. During the winter months, this is prime eagle viewing territory between the "Fort" and BLM land at .9 mile with a wetlands pond on your right and day area on your left. I have seen up to seven eagles on a single outing. This is also a favorite area of ducks, Canadian geese, and an occasional blue heron.

Cross a bridge constructed of recycled plastic to an intersection with a private road do not turn left (private property), stay right, go up hill; the concrete trail is replaced by the road for 650 feet where it is reborn at the top, 8 minutes into the ride. **1.3 mile mark:** elevation 6880.

Follow the trail as it runs between the Uncompahgre River and Highway 550 until you reach County Rd. 24 and the south entrance of Ridgway State Park **2.5 mile mark:** elevation 6870, 15 minutes. Enter the Park, follow the path all the way to the dam, 6.5 miles farther.

2.9 mile mark: bridge to your left crossing the Uncompahgre River connects with an short trail on the west side. Good area for spotting Canadian geese, ducks, and blue herons.

3.7 mile mark: trail turns slightly east and the entire reservoir comes into view. Stay left and close to the reservoir when meeting any junctions.

4.3 mile mark: elevation 6740; 25-30 minutes. Lake view parking lot; you can see the dam off to your left, north. Follow the concrete trail until it turns to a gravel trail that begins to circumnavigate the reservoir and parallels a deer fence on your right which keeps deer out of harms way. Begin a gentle climb which gradually increases in difficulty.

4.9 mile mark: steep, short stretch followed by another. Trail is narrow so keep in mind the sharp dropoffs.

5.0 mile mark: elevation 6950; 40 minutes. Continue on, endure the tough switchbacks in the climb to the top/ Visitor's Center or what was known as Enchanted Mesa before it became the park.

5.1 mile mark: elevation 6940; 43 minutes. T-intersection to the right is the Visitor's Center, Park Headquarters. Continue on our ride to the left, come to a sign - "Dutch Charlie", continue to the right. To the left takes you up to Elk Ridge Campground, the Wapiti Trail, which is higher up on the mesa. Go across paved road, brown sign - "Piñon Park Trail"; follow it down until you reach the swim beach and marina; .6 mile, elevation 6980.

5.8 mile mark: elevation 6890; 50 minutes. Junction, to the left is Secret Spot Trail, leading to picnic area and cove overlook, .2 mile. Turn right into parking lot and follow it to the southeast side of swim beach. Go into day use area south of swim beach and by the children's playground equipment. Look for the trail along a wooden fence heading east; take this trail. As it circumnavigates the cove, it becomes a dirt trail, then back on concrete to picnic tables on a circular drive.

6.4 mile mark: "Meirs Bay Trail" (on a brown sign) connects to Enchanted Mesa Trail to dam; continue around bay.

7 mile mark: elevation 6780; 60 minutes. Directly across from swim beach.

7.3 mile mark: elevation 6790; end of concrete, very steep.

7.6 mile mark: elevation 6950; above reservoir, some steep dropouts.

8 mile mark: elevation 6940; 75 minutes. Cross a wooden bridge; be cautious.

9 mile mark: 1.5 hours; north of dam. Can see the spillway. Come to a sign that says "Steep Grades, Tight Turns," this descends to the Pa-Co-Chu-Puk recreation site camping and day use area. Future plans call for the trail to continue around the west side of the reservoir, but for now reverse and return to Ridgway. Final elevation is 6960. This ride offers great views of the Sneffels Range, Ridgway Reservoir, and Loghill Mesa. Return trip is 1.25 hours; total 2.5-3 hours, 18 miles round trip.

ॐ